PERGAMON INTERNATIONAL LIBRARY
of Science, Technology, Engineering and Social Studies
*The 1000-volume original paperback library in aid of education,
industrial training and the enjoyment of leisure*
Publisher: Robert Maxwell, M.C.

GLOBAL DIALOGUE

The New International Economic Order

Courtesy Angel Zamarripa

GLOBAL DIALOGUE

The New International Economic Order

B. P. MENON

Centre for Economic & Social Information, The United Nations, New York

PERGAMON PRESS

OXFORD · NEW YORK · TORONTO · SYDNEY · PARIS · FRANKFURT

U.K.	Pergamon Press Ltd., Headington Hill Hall, Oxford OX3 0BW, England
U.S.A.	Pergamon Press Inc., Maxwell House, Fairview Park, Elmsford, New York 10523, U.S.A.
CANADA	Pergamon of Canada Ltd., 75 The East Mall, Toronto, Ontario, Canada
AUSTRALIA	Pergamon Press (Aust.) Pty. Ltd., 19a Boundary Street, Rushcutters Bay, N.S.W. 2011, Australia
FRANCE	Pergamon Press SARL, 24 Rue des Ecoles, 75240 Paris, Cedex 05, France
WEST GERMANY	Pergamon Press GmbH, 6242 Kronberg-Taunus, Pferdstrasse 1, Frankfurt-am-Main, West Germany

First edition 1977

Library of Congress Cataloging in Publication Data

Menon, Bhaskar P
Global Dialogue

(Pergamon international library of science, technology, engineering, and social studies)
1. Economic history—1945-   2. International economic relations. 3. Underdeveloped areas. I. Title.
HC59.M445 1977   382.1   77-1644

ISBN 0-08-021498-3
ISBN 0-08-021499-1 pbk.

Printed in Great Britain by Butler & Tanner Ltd, Frome and London

CONTENTS

ACKNOWLEDGEMENTS

In writing this book I drew on the work of many other United Nations staff members, the anonymous authors of expert reports and studies. The chapter on Multinational Trade Negotiations, in particular, is heavily in debt to UNCTAD reports to the General Assembly. People I can thank by name are Harry Lennon, Steve Whitehouse and Bill Lineberry, all colleagues; and Geeta Khale and Fenwick Anderson, student interns with CESI when the book was being written.

Others to thank are the cartoonists whose work spices this book. The cartoons were selected from countries around the world by United Nations Information Centres. The cartoonists are:

Front cover — Victor Monge (VIC) in the Nacional, Mexico.

Frontispiece — Angel Zamarripa (FACHA) in Jueves de Excelsior, Mexico.

Pages 6 and 59 — Murray Ball in One World, United Kingdom.

Page 9 — R. K. Laxman in the Times of India.

Page 17 — Pat Porter in Development Forum, a CESI publication.

Pages 21, 31, 55 — Jean Plantureux (PLANTU) in Le Monde, France.

Pages 24, 51 — Zarko Karabatic. Unpublished. © Karabatic.

Page 39 — Salih Memecsn in Baris, Turkey.

Page 45 — ACB in a World Development Movement Publication, United Kingdom.

Page 65 — Terry Hirst in Joe Magazine, Kenya.

Page 77 — Angelo Lodigiani (LOD) for ASCA, Italy.

Page 83 — E. Gurova in Crocodil, the Soviet Union.

CHAPTER I

THE ECONOMIC SCENE

During the past few years newspaper editors around the world have had to contend with a startling new development. They have seen stories on international economics leap from the grey monotony of their financial pages and jostle from the headlines the more familiar dramas of daily journalism. But though these stories of currency rates, wheat deals and oil politics are read by millions, international economics remains for most people a dim and mysterious area. And recent events have done little to clear the public view. As efforts to deal with the roiled world economy have intensified and negotiations got under way to create a new international economic order, a fog of Declarations, Conventions, Plans and Programmes has issued from a lengthening series of international meetings. Individually their reasons and purposes are clear; but together they threaten to overwhelm the understanding. Where do they all point? How do they fit together? What do they intend?

There are, of course, no simple and pat answers to these questions. What this booklet offers is a basic sketch of the emerging scene: a line-drawing of the economic landscape and a guide to where the smoke signals are coming from and why.

THE BASIC FACTS

The world today is made up of over 150 nation states, of which 144 are members of the United Nations. There are over four billion (4,000,000,000) people on earth now and, growing at the rate of 1.9 per cent per year, this number is expected to double by the year 2010. Human knowledge too is growing at an explosive rate, the sum total doubling, it is estimated, every decade. Increasingly the forces of science and technology shape

1

traditional societies, and all cultures and value systems are forced to adapt to a shrinking, ever more interdependent world. These and many other factors, quite without precedent in human history, form the backdrop of international negotiations today. Increasingly they are the imperatives that prompt and guide these negotiations.

The basic economic and social problem the United Nations has faced during the last three decades is that of global poverty. Some two-thirds of the world's people are poor. Millions of them live in perpetual hunger, many millions are killed and crippled by diseases that have been curable for years. Their children grow up illiterate, minds and bodies stunted from lack of food. From generation to generation they endure conditions that stifle all the great human potential in them, existing as marginal people in a brutal world. Little touched by science and technology, this two-thirds of humanity offers a stark and shocking contrast to the other— affluent—third.

CLOSING THE GAP

Efforts to close the gap between the world's rich and poor have been continuous over the past 30 years but, for a variety of reasons, there has been little success. Analyses of this experience led the "developing" countries to conclude that though their situations and problems differed widely, they did share one overwhelming problem: a system of global rules and practices that worked consistently against their interests. This perception led to a call by the United Nations General Assembly, at a special session in June 1974, for the creation of a "New International Economic Order". Although several developed countries said they did not agree with all the provisions of the Assembly resolution, it was adopted by consensus, along with a "Programme of Action".

The reasons for the call for a new order were summed up by Secretary-General Waldheim when he said in a speech in early 1975:

"Many new nations, having won political independence, find themselves still bound by economic dependency. For a long time it was thought that the solution to this problem was aid and assistance. It is increasingly clear, however, that a New International Economic Order is essential if the relations between the rich and poor nations are to be transformed into a mutually beneficial partnership. Otherwise the existing gap between these groups of nations will increasingly represent a potential threat to international peace and security.

"Moreover [the Secretary-General continued] the dependence of the developing world upon the developed is changing—indeed, in certain cases has been reversed. Many developed nations are also finding themselves in serious economic difficulties. The international system of economic and trade relations which was devised 30 years ago is now manifestly inadequate for the needs of the world community as a whole. The charge against that order in the past was that it worked well for the affluent and against the poor. It cannot now even be said that it works well for the affluent."

The essence of the new order demanded by the developing countries is simply their "full and complete economic emancipation". And the way to achieve this they agreed (at a Conference of Developing Countries in Dakar in early 1975), was "to recover and control their natural resources and wealth, and the means of economic development". They would "change their traditional approach to negotiations with developed countries, hitherto consisting in the presentation of a list of requests to developed countries and an appeal to their political goodwill which in reality was seldom forthcoming". The new approach to negotiations would involve common action to strengthen their bargaining position, more economic activity among themselves and a strategy based on "the principle of relying first and foremost on themselves".

The General Assembly followed its call for the establishment of a New International Economic Order with the adoption, in December 1974, of a Charter of Economic Rights and Duties of States. This Charter complements the earlier document in the sense that it sets out for the first time a set of principles and guidelines to govern economic behaviour at the national level. As with the earlier resolution, several developed countries had strong reservations on the Charter and they voted against it, but the majority accepted the principles and guidelines as the basis of their attempts to create a new international economic order.

The representatives of developing countries have stressed repeatedly that the approach to a new international economic order would have to be comprehensive and not piecemeal. It should be based on the right of nations to control and expropriate foreign owned property and enterprises in accordance with national laws. It should involve the transfer of more resources to developing countries, as well as a "code of conduct" for the transfer of technology. It would require the restructuring of many international institutions and the rearranging of the world monetary and financial systems. It implies not only the stabilization of commodity prices at equitable levels, but also a linking or "indexing" of these prices to those of manufactured goods.

These demands for comprehensive change came at a time of widespread economic crisis, and the initial reaction of the most powerful developed countries was negative. But during the year that followed there was a general attempt to re-examine old positions. There was wide recognition that a common crisis could only be solved by co-operative action. The result was evident when the General Assembly of the United Nations met again in special session in September 1975, and this is the topic of the next chapter.

CHAPTER II

THE SEVENTH SPECIAL SESSION

The Seventh Special Session of the United Nations General Assembly met, literally, at two levels. At the upper level, in the gold-domed grandeur of the Assembly Hall, delegates listened to the slow unfolding of the formal debate. The proceedings here went strictly by tradition and rule, with Algerian Foreign Minister Abdelaziz Bouteflika presiding from the green marble podium as representatives of 108 countries outlined their views and proposals on development and economic co-operation. Meanwhile, in the basement directly under the Assembly floor, work proceeded at a different pace. In small conference rooms blue with cigarette smoke, delegates met in closed sessions to haggle and argue over the issues dividing them. Here there was little formality to begin with, and as negotiations wore through long days and ever later into the nights, all unnecessary frills disappeared. Jackets were slung over the backs of chairs, shirt sleeves were rolled up, ties loosened, and voices rasped increasingly with fatigue and, occasionally, irritation.

THE GENERAL DEBATE

Before the opening of the general debate there were two keynote speeches of major significance by the President of the Assembly and by the Secretary-General of the United Nations.

The speech of the Assembly President, Mr. Bouteflika, recalled the reverberations of the last Special Session, held at his country's initiative in the spring of 1974. That strident session had called, despite the reservations of major developed countries, for a New International Economic Order. And Mr. Bouteflika echoed this demand in a speech that touched on the whole range of changes developing countries want in the global economy. It had become clear, said Mr. Bouteflika, "that the prosperity of the West is derived to a large extent from the draining of the wealth and exploitation of the labour of the peoples of the third world, and that their economic apparatus, imposing though it be, rests on fragile and vulnerable foundations". The Sixth Special Session of the Assembly, he said, had marked the international community's recognition of the "true nature and magnitude of the problems of development". There was awareness now that in a complex and interdependent world economy it was no longer possible for anyone to impose solutions of his own choice.

'ONE WORLD

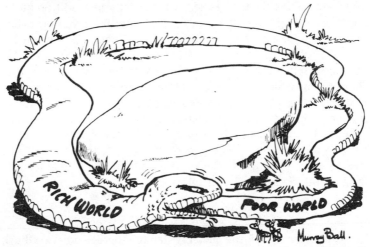

Courtesy Murray Ball

The Seventh Special Session, Mr. Bouteflika continued, "confronts each one of us with historic responsibilities. What kind of world do we want to build? What kind of future are we to prepare for coming generations? These questions must be given an unequivocal answer..." The developing countries, he said, had proposed a pattern of co-operation that would allow countries to build their economies on the "foundation of their own resources and make international trade the favoured instrument of an equitable world distribution of world income". Calling on industrialized nations to demonstrate clearly their will for practical co-operation, Mr. Bouteflika said that in the quest for new relationships the first step would be "for the more fortunate to make the necessary concessions and yield to the legitimate aspirations of those to whom history, and sometimes nature, have been ungenerous". He called on the Assembly to adopt measures to solve the most pressing problems now and establish the framework and objectives for long-term negotiations.

In a speech immediately after that of the Assembly President, Secretary-General Kurt Waldheim focussed on the role of the United Nations in the "long process" of global development. Reviewing the variety of United Nations attempts to further development, the Secretary-General said they revealed "an ever accelerating evolution of the concept of international co-responsibility and interdependence, from a rather abstract idea to one which is today universally acknowledged as a practical necessity". The reduction of the gap between the world's rich and poor was, he said, "the greatest challenge" to international statesmanship and vision. "It is the experience of history that no society, in which the few have wealth and the majority live in poverty and without hope, can remain stable. This is more than ever true of our world society today".

It was encouraging that so many governmental and non-governmental forums had been dealing with this problem, the Secretary-General went on. "It is certainly a reflection of the seriousness of the situation, but I believe it is also an indication that we are dealing with an idea whose time has come." While discussions in other forums could contribute significantly to the negotiating process, the Secretary-General said, the role of the United Nations was unique in that it was "universal in character, comprehensive in its scope of responsibility and enduring in its concern with international issues".

Mr. Waldheim identified three functions which the United Nations should perform in the mix of interacting events within and outside the Organization:

"First, through this Assembly, the United Nations should provide the blueprint, framework and guidelines for the negotiating process which will ensue both within and outside the United Nations system.

"Second, the results of these negotiations should be brought before the General Assembly in order to give such agreements the confirmation which only a universal organization can provide.

"Finally, the United Nations is particularly suited to providing continuity by monitoring and following up on agreements reached by the international community."

The general debate that followed these speeches lasted for ten days and 22 meetings of the plenary. The debate covered in detail and from a variety of angles the main themes of concern to the international community. It was, as the representative of Mauritius said on the eighth day, "unlike any other debate in the General Assembly" in that "this one has been a genuine conversation amongst nations. New ideas have been introduced and expanded upon, delegations have listened to each other in earnest dialogue."

Despite its diversity and range, however, the general debate followed the main lines defined by the Economic and Social Council at its 59th session.* The Council had recommended that attention be given to six major areas of global concern:

(1) International trade;
(2) Transfer of resources to finance development and international monetary reform;
(3) Science and technology;
(4) Industrialization;
(5) Agricultural development;
(6) Restructuring of the United Nations system.

In each of these areas, the developing countries perceived a situation unfairly biased against them. As the Brazilian Minister for External Relations observed, there existed "two levels of relationships" in international affairs. "At one level, that of the economic relations among industrialized countries, there exists a relatively effective framework of rules capable of disciplining over-all developments with a view towards that harmonious development which the majority of these countries are already achieving internally.... At another level, [in] relations between developed and developing countries ... a virtual *laissez faire* prevails ... an order which results, in practice, in the subordination of the economically strong."

The Foreign Minister of Iran struck the same note when he said: "There is hardly any major manufactured produce in the western world in the sale of which some tacit understanding or oligopolistic behaviour does

---

*Economic and Social Council resolution 1980 (LIX), adopted 31 July 1975.

not exist among principal sellers. Even with regard to basic food, upon which the survival of man depends, for years, as now admitted, the agricultural policies of the major exporting nations were based on the premise that production to full capacity created undesirable surpluses and depressed markets. It is ironic that by a curious logic the fixing of oil prices by the major oil companies in the past was not considered a cartel action, and yet today the setting of prices by oil producing nations in the exercise of their sovereign rights is so harshly criticized."

In answer to the demands by developing countries that a new order be introduced in international economic affairs, the Foreign Minister of the Federal Republic of Germany reflected the position of several major developed countries when he said: "This complex task can be solved only with the help of the steering principle of the free market." It would be "utopian and dangerous" to attempt a solution by "international dirigism", he said, and "any attempt to do so could end up only in paralysis and a wastage of resources".

Courtesy R. K. Laxman

Philosophical and technical differences tended to concentrate on what the Foreign Minister of India termed the "two main pillars" of international co-operation for development: aid and trade. "Not only have the targets for aid set in the International Development Strategy not been reached," he said, "but there has been a gradual contraction in real terms." Referring to the demand by developing countries for a "link" between the creation of new international reserve assets (namely, SDRs) and development assistance, the Foreign Minister pointed out that "less than 4 per cent of the additional liquidity created in the past two decades has accrued to developing countries which account for 70 per cent of the world's population". As for trade, the Indian Minister said that prices of most commodities exported by developing countries remained either depressed or unstable. "The import bills of most developing countries have increased to such an extent that even with a 100 per cent increase in export earnings there is no assurance that the imbalance will be corrected or even met half way," he said.

While the substantive elements of difference in the debate were not new, there was an altogether new mood of conciliation that prevailed in the Assembly. This was reflected in almost every statement but it received most attention in the speech delivered on behalf of the United States Secretary of State. In the speech, the United States representative summed up the reason for the new mood in the Assembly when he said: "The global order of colonial power that lasted through centuries has now disappeared; the cold war division of the world into two rigid blocs has now also broken down and major changes have taken place in the international economy. We now live in a world of some 150 nations. We live in an environment of continuing conflicts, proliferating weapons, new ideological divisions and economic rivalry. The developing nations have stated their claim for a greater role, for more control over their economic destiny and for a just share in global prosperity. The economically advanced nations have stated their claim for reliable supplies of energy, raw materials and other products at a fair price; they seek stable economic relationships and expanding world trade, for these are important to the well-being of their own societies."

The same conciliatory note was struck by the Italian spokesman who said on behalf of the entire European Economic Community: "The time has come to recognize that monetary stability and order, secure conditions for trade and international investments, a balanced distribution of resources—and thus political and social stability—are interdependent objectives which cannot be achieved without a new, better balanced, wiser and fairer international economic order."

Socialist countries which were, in the words of the Soviet Ambassador, the "natural allies" of developing countries, also added to the mood. "The present political situation in the world is particularly favourable for the solution of these problems", said the representative of the USSR. "It is characterized by the continuing relaxation of tension, the diminishing danger of war and the affirmation of the principles of peaceful coexistence in international relations. To make political *détente* an irreversible process and to complement it by military *détente*, to take real steps towards limiting the nuclear arms race and averting a nuclear war, to reduce and, subsequently, end the arms race while working for general and complete disarmament is the order of the day." ·

THE NEGOTIATIONS

The negotiations in the basement conference rooms of the Assembly were between "contact groups". In main, they were between the 27-member contact group of the Group of 77 (developing countries) and the 12-member contact group of Western European and Other countries (WEO). This was as much because the socialist countries of Eastern Europe and China supported the position of the developing countries as it was because they did not play a major part in those aspects of the international economy which the developing countries want changed. As the Foreign Minister of the Federal Republic of Germany said, "Out of the total exports of the developing countries, 75 per cent are absorbed by the Organization for Economic Co-operation and Development (OECD) countries alone, 20 per cent constitute exchanges among the developing countries themselves, and 5 per cent go to countries with centrally planned economies. This means the growth rates of the industrialized countries with free market economies and those of the developing countries are inseparably linked with each other."

Negotiations between the contact groups of the developing and the WEO countries were entirely in closed sessions. One set of negotiators met on the major problem areas of trade and transfer of resources; a second set worked on the other four items of the agenda, industrialization, science and technology, food and agriculture, and restructuring of the United Nations. The position of the European Community on major sections of the basic working paper tabled by the Group of 77 had already been subject to some negotiations during the preparatory phase of the Special Session. The United States' position, articulated as it was for the first time on the opening day of the conference, and containing as it did so many proposals, presented a major task for the negotiators.

As the first week passed and then the second, differences narrowed but not enough to warrant a full consensus. The scheduled end of the session came and went but the negotiations continued. They continued over the week-end of 13 September, continued all day and night on Monday. Finally, in the early dawn of Tuesday the bleary-eyed delegates reached agreement.

THE RESULTS

The resolution they finally adopted without a vote on 16 September runs to some 7,000 words. Its language would not get high marks for elegance anywhere, but the hard slogging prose does manage to carry the weight of a complex and difficult consensus. The resolution consists of seven sections:

International trade;
Transfer of resources for development;
Science and technology;
Industrialization;
Food and agriculture;
Cooperation among developing countries;
Restructuring the United Nations system.

There was no complete agreement on all points in the resolution, for the United States, some members of the European Community and Japan expressed reservations on their ability to meet the targets set for developmental aid. The United States also expressed reservation on several other points, including indexation of commodity prices to the prices of manufactured goods and the proposed "link" between the creation of SDRs and development assistance. But over all, there was agreement, and this was reflected in the final statement of the United States Ambassador, whose delegation had expressed the most reservations. "Perhaps never in the history of the United Nations," he said, "has there been so intensive and so genuine a negotiation among so many nations on so profoundly important a range of issues. We have shown that we can negotiate in good faith and, in doing so, reach genuine accord. Not least, we have shown that this can be done in the unique and indispensable setting of the United Nations. The system works."

Secretary-General Waldheim underscored the significance of the agreement when he said: "The first stage of a constructive and realistic compact of policies and measures has been achieved....After having established last year the principles for a new economic order, this session has tackled in a practical way the key elements of such a new order. We all knew that during a period of two weeks we would not be able to solve all the problems we are faced with, but I think we all note with great satisfaction that it was possible to start a negotiating process which led to most important decisions. What is necessary now is to...translate them into concrete agreements in the period ahead." And Jan Pronk, the Dutch Chairman of the main negotiating committee, also looked to the future when he commented wearily to press correspondents after the close of the session that there was essentially a "commitment to commit" efforts towards change. Because of the political atmosphere in which the consensus had been reached, said Mr. Pronk, the Special Session "was quite an important happening". As a result of it, future negotiations, including and especially those at the UN Conference on Trade and Development in Nairobi (see Chapter IV), would be "different" from what they would otherwise have been.

CHAPTER III

REVIEWING THE LAST HALF-DECADE

The same day that the Seventh Special Session of the General Assembly ended in New York, its outgoing President called to order the 30th regular session of the Assembly. The regular session had an extensive agenda of 126 items ranging over every aspect of international affairs, but one in particular had direct relevance to the special session and the negotiations it initiated. This was agenda item 65, titled "Mid-term review and appraisal of progress in the implementation of the International Development Strategy for the Second United Nations Development Decade". It allowed the delegates a chance to look back at what had happened during the first five years of the seventies and consider how far the strategy they had worked out in the late sixties had succeeded.

The review took place, the Assembly noted in the resolution it finally adopted, "at a time when the international economic situation is continuing to change and when events have been following each other so rapidly as to shake the foundations of the existing economic order. In the first half of the Decade there has been a succession of crucial events. The Bretton Woods system* broke down in 1971. From January 1973 the prices of food, fuel and fertilizer rose so rapidly that, together with ever increasing prices of capital goods, equipment and services the balance of payments situation of most developing countries deteriorated".

The Assembly noted that during 1974 most commodity prices had slumped and existing "structural imbalances" in agricultural production had been aggravated by a continuation of unfavourable climatic conditions. The situation in developing countries was further exacerbated by

---

*The monetary system governing the world's market economies that resulted from consultations held at Bretton Woods in the United States after World War II.

the economic recession in the developed market economies, combined with the acceleration of the pace of inflation. During the first half of the Decade, an alarming increase occurred in the gap between developed and developing countries". The gloomy picture was lightened by one element, which the Assembly also noted: "there was an irreversible and most promising change in the relationship of forces of the world. The developing countries emerged as a more powerful factor, as a necessary consequence of the new and growing perception of the reality of interdependence."

Analysing the events of the last five years in more detail, the Assembly noted that developed countries had not, "by and large, implemented the policy measures of the International Development Strategy, and indeed there has been some retrogression". Despite this, though, "some of the aggregate targets set in the International Development Strategy were met or exceeded, owing mainly to the developing countries' own efforts and to a certain extent to external factors such as the commodity boom"; (a short-lived rise in commodity prices between 1972 and 1974). These aggregates did not reflect the variation in achievement among developing countries, the Assembly noted, for many countries did much worse than the average figures would indicate.

The main feature of achievement during the half-decade are summed up in the following comparative figures:

The average growth rate in developing countries continued at approximately the target set for the Decade, though the annual growth rate *per capita* was 3.3 per cent, or a little below the target of 3.5 per cent set by the International Development Strategy.

TABLE 1
GROSS DOMESTIC PRODUCT OF DEVELOPING COUNTRIES
(International Development Strategy target, 1971-1980:
6 per cent per annum)

Average Annual Rate of Change (percentage)		Percentage Change from Preceding Year			
1961-1970	1971-1974	1971	1972	1973	1974
5.5	5.9	5.2	5.6	7.0	5.6

Source: *World Economic Survey, 1974* (United Nations publication, Sales No. E.75. II.C.1).

A major area of shortfall was in the agricultural sector, where less than half the target rate of 4 per cent was realized by the developing countries as a whole.

TABLE 2
AGRICULTURAL PRODUCTION OF DEVELOPING COUNTRIES
(International Development Strategy target, 1971-1980:
4 per cent per annum)

Average Annual Rate of Change (percentage)		Percentage Change from Preceding Year			
1961-1970	1971-1974	1971	1972	1973	1974
2.8	1.5	1.6	-0.8	3.9	1.5

Source: *World Economic Survey, 1974.*

The over-all target of 8 per cent per annum in manufacturing output was attained in general, and in some cases exceeded.

TABLE 3
MANUFACTURING PRODUCTION OF DEVELOPING COUNTRIES
(International Development Strategy target, 1971-1980:
8 per cent per annum)

Average Annual Rate of Change (percentage)	Percentage Change from Preceding Year			
1971-1974	1971	1972	1973	1974
8.3	6.7	8.9	9.0	8.7

Source: *World Economic Survey, 1974.*

Developing countries as a whole achieved the domestic savings rate of 20 per cent set for 1980, though for many developing countries the rate was somewhat less.

A main factor conducive to the over-all achievements of the developing countries during this period was trade. In external trade and payments, quantum increases for many developing countries in the early years of the Decade decelerated in 1974, resulting in an average rate of somewhat less than the 7 per cent target of the International Development Strategy.

TABLE 4
CHANGE IN EXPORTS AND IMPORTS OF DEVELOPING COUNTRIES
(International Development Strategy target, 1971-1980:
7 per cent per annum)

Average Annual Rate of Increase		Percentage Change from Preceding Year			
	1971-1974	1971	1972	1973	1974
Quantum of exports	6.5	7.1	8.4	8.3	2.5
Quantum of imports	7.9	7.1	1.9	9.8	13.1

Source: *World Economic Survey, 1974.*

The net flow of financial resources in the form of official development assistance decreased in real terms and as a percentage of gross national product.

Courtesy Pat Porter

TABLE 5
NET FLOW OF OFFICIAL DOMESTIC ASSISTANCE FROM
DEVELOPED MARKET ECONOMY COUNTRIES
(International Development Strategy target, 1971-1980:
0:7 per cent per annum)

Period		
1969-1970	1971-1973	1974[a]
0.34	0.32	0.32

Source: *World Economic Survey, 1974.*
[a]Provisional data.

The burden of debt service payments of developing countries continued to increase in relation to their export earnings.

TABLE 6.

SERVICE PAYMENTS ON EXTERNAL PUBLIC DEBT OF
SEVENTY-EIGHT DEVELOPING COUNTRIES

	Percentage share of public debt service payment to the exports of goods and non-factor services (seventy-eight developing countries)
1967	9.9
1970	11.2
1973	10.9

Source: Centre for Development Planning, Projections and Policies of the United Nations Secretariat.

Population policies have, by and large, been implemented by developing countries within the context of their development plans and priorities, and the target of 2.5 per cent of average annual increase in population in developing countries has almost been reached.

At its 31st session the U.N. General Assembly again considered developments relevant to the International Development Strategy. It noted "the regret expressed by the developing countries that the developed countries have yet to display the necessary political will". And in a long sentence it detailed the woes of the developing countries: "During the current Second U.N. Development Decade the terms of trade of the majority of developing countries have deteriorated . . . they have unprecedented and growing balance of payments deficits . . . the burden of debt has reached unmanageable proportions in many developing countries and growth in the developing countries is expected to fall short not only of the 6 per cent target of the International Development Strategy but also of the rate of growth achieved in the First U.N. Development Decade . . . for many developing countries, particularly among the least developed, land-locked, island and most seriously affected developing countries, real per capita income could, if present trends persist, be lower in 1980 than at the start of the Decade."

In another resolution the General Assembly called for a full debate during its 1977 session on plans for a new Strategy based on the "need to introduce profound changes in economic relations between the developed and developing countries". It asked the U.N. Secretary-General to submit studies and reports containing all relevant information for this purpose.

CHAPTER IV

THE UNITED NATIONS CONFERENCE ON TRADE AND DEVELOPMENT: UNCTAD IV

Eight months after the Seventh Special Session of the United Nations General Assembly drew up its large prescription for global well-being, UNCTAD IV met in Nairobi to try and produce some therapeutic pills for specific ailments. There was intense interest in how the conference would go, for during its 12-year history UNCTAD had built a reputation as the forum where diplomats bared their souls. How would the changed international atmosphere, betokened by the "mood of conciliation" at the Seventh Special Session affect the proceedings in Nairobi? Would the frank statistical warfare of the earlier UNCTAD sessions give way to true negotiations?

The conference met in the Kenyatta Centre, the round tower of which rises into the always dramatic Kenyan sky, the highest building in the country. Beside it, and part of the same steel and concrete complex, is a conference hall built to look like a village hut. Irreverent journalists—there were some 500 in attendance—saw this as symbolic of the transformation of the Third World in international relations; they also saw omens in the fact that the week before the conference met, the plenary hall had been the site of a series of boxing matches. But the fourth UNCTAD differed from its predecessors in not being the usual boxing match between the world's poor and rich. And there were a variety of reasons for this.

Unlike its predecessors, UNCTAD IV was planned and structured for efficient decision-making. Where the first three sessions had lasted anywhere from two to four months and held vociferous debates on some 40 different agenda items, the Nairobi session was only four weeks long and had only eight substantive items on its agenda. There was general debate

only in the plenary and all negotiations were in closed sessions where
there was minimal temptation to play to the gallery. (This was possible,
in a way, because the preceding UNCTAD sessions had served their purpose in raising global consciousness about issues by debating them publicly and at length.) The fourth session also had the advantage of meeting in an international economic climate much changed by the squalls
and cyclones of the early seventies. The rich were sensitive as never before to their vulnerability in an interdependent world; the poor were
freshly aware of their potential strength.

The conference began with the usual round of formal speeches,
Kenyan President Jomo Kenyatta sending Minister of State Mbiu
Koinange to do the honors on behalf of the host country, followed by
Secretary-General Kurt Waldheim and then UNCTAD Secretary-General
Gamani Corea. Mr. Waldheim, blinking in the glare of television arc
lamps, minced no words when he described the task before the meeting:
"The achievement of political independence does not represent the end
of the struggle. We are now engaged upon the achievement of economic
decolonization, and upon the creation of a new international economic
order. In a very real sense this is a liberation movement—liberation for
the masses of humanity from poverty, hunger, unemployment and de-
spair."

UNCTAD Secretary-General Gamani Corea, an economist from Sri
Lanka who has headed the organization for the last two years, sketched
in more detail, highlighting the mechanics of liberation. The conference,
he said, was a vital link in the international community's attempt to
translate general agreements reached in the United Nations General
Assembly into specific programmes for action. Failure to do so would
"not only aggravate but actually foster crises and tensions, turmoil and
turbulence throughout many parts of the world".

There has never before been such an acute recognition that development is a political issue, Mr. Corea said. And this needed to be matched
with "a parallel recognition that this issue cannot be resolved effectively
and rapidly, without some basic changes in prevailing structures and prevailing relationships. It cannot be solved by the mere interplay of the invisible forces of the market. Nor can it be solved by financial transfers
alone, leaving the fabric of prevailing international economic relations
unchanged".

Courtesy Jean Plantureux

The existing order of economic relationships in the world, he went on, was "inadequate during its heyday. It is still less adequate at the present time when it is itself in deep crisis." In illustration he quoted some figures. From 1952 to 1972 the total GNP of developed market economies had increased from $1,250 billion to $3,000 billion. The increase alone was three and a half times the total GNP of developing countries. For individuals in the two groups of countries the implication of this was even more striking. Where the average person in the developed countries saw his income grow from $2,000 per year in 1952 to $4,000 in 1972, the increase in developing countries was a meagre $125—rising from $175 to $300. In stark physical terms this meant that in the developing countries today "some 300 million people...are unemployed or underemployed... about 700 million are living in destitution and almost 500 million are suffering from severe protein malnutrition".

The reason why the swift growth of developed countries had so little effect on the growth of the developing countries Mr. Corea said, was that there were "weaknesses in the mechanisms" linking the two groups. These weaknesses were in the areas of trade in commodities and manufactures, and in the ways in which technology and financial resources were made available to developing countries. "If the prevailing order has to be changed,"said Mr. Corea, "it has to be changed in each of these areas. This is the main lesson to be learned from the decades that have gone by since the second world war".

Speaking after Mr. Corea, President Ferdinand Marcos of the Phillippines took a longer view. In a speech of sustained eloquence he looked back to the earliest known origins of man in the great rift valley in East Africa, the country around the conference site itself. "Since man first appeared on this planet the human species has always had to contend for survival," he said. "Man had to break away from the jungle, make his home away from the beasts of the forest and seek the society of his own kind. Here he learned the joys of living, here also he came to know of hunger, disease, solitude and war.

"In nearly two million years he has populated the earth close to bursting point. To it he has brought great suffering and want. Some of us have learned to accept what we have suffered, but no one accepts the misery we are further called upon to endure."

Looking to more recent history the President of the Philippines warned of confrontation between the world's poor and rich if existing trends continued. "A decade and a half ago," he said, "all our countries joined in declaring the sixties—in the same manner that we declared the seventies—a Decade for Development. This occasioned much confidence in a world-wide effort and a general advance in which the developing peoples would finally share in the earth's abundance. But in the interval there developed a gap between expectation and fulfilment..."

Since UNCTAD first met 12 years ago in Geneva, Mr. Marcos said, the world has changed. "From the grim awareness of the intolerable contradiction of want in the midst of plenty, and unprecedented knowledge in the midst of ignorance...we have now reached the equally grim prospects of unwanted protracted confrontation over these problems." It would be "folly" to insist, said Mr. Marcos, that the developing countries had not developed the collective capacity to act.

Introducing the Manila Declaration and Programme of Action setting forth the position of developing countries in their negotiations with the developed countries, Mr. Marcos warned that it should not be misunderstood. "The Manila Declaration is not a litany of sins," he said. "It is not a one-sided enunciation of grievances. It is a brief and candid listing of what the developing nations believe to be the most urgent problems... it gives what we submit are just and reasonable solutions...."

THE ISSUES

The Manila Declaration and Programme of Action touched on all the items before the conference: on commodity trade (upon which the majority of developing countries are heavily dependent for income); on trade in manufactures and semi-manufactures (upon which lie their hopes for accelerated economic diversification and development); on science and technology; on the availability of financial resources; on co-operation among developing countries; on trade relations between countries with different economic and social systems; on special measures for the least developed, the land-locked and the island developing countries; and on institutional matters affecting UNCTAD itself.

The Manila Declaration and Programme of Action contained proposals for an integrated programme for commodities which aimed, *inter alia*, to improve the terms of trade of developing countries, to support prices of commodities to remunerative and just levels for producers and equitable to consumers, to reduce excessive fluctuations in commodity prices and supplies and to improve and stabilize the real purchasing power of the export earnings of developing countries. The programme provided for safeguards for countries that were either net importers of commodities or were geographically disadvantaged and thus incapable of making full use of their resources. The key element of the integrated programme—a common fund that would act as a bank to finance buffer stocks of a range of selected commodities—became the focus of attention early in the debate in Nairobi.

The Manila programme also included a section on manufactures and semi-manufactures setting out a comprehensive strategy to expand and diversify the export trade of developing countries. Another section referred to multilateral trade negotiations, progress in which had been disappointing for the developing countries. Specific measures in this field, contained in the Manila Declaration and Programme of Action, included a request that immediate consideration be given to reforming the provisions of GATT, in order to provide, on a mandatory basis, for differentiated and more favourable treatment to developing countries. The over-all target in this area is the increase of the developing countries' share of world industrial output to 25 per cent by the year 2000.

Another important section of the proposals dealt with the transfer of financial resources to developing countries, particularly with the alleviation of the crushing burden of debt borne by many poor countries.

Courtesy Zarko Karabatic

The 77 saw their separate debt problems as springing from the system of international economic relations in which they were such unequal and disadvantaged partners. To deal with shared problems and to lay down guidelines for the treatment of international debt, the 77 called for a conference under the aegis of UNCTAD that would implement the principles and guidelines on the renegotiation of official and commercial debts to be reached at UNCTAD IV. Specific proposals put forward by the 77 included the writing off of the official debt of the least developed countries, the developing land-locked and the developing island countries; for other most seriously affected countries, it was proposed to waive service payments on official debts until these countries cease to be regarded by the United Nations as "Most Seriously Affected". Neither developed market economy countries nor indeed the socialist countries of Eastern Europe considered these ideas with much enthusiasm.

The Manila Declaration and Programme of Action dealt also with questions of Transfer of Technology, proposing specific action to strengthen the technological capacity of developing countries, including the formulation of a code of conduct for the transfer of technology and actions to be undertaken by UNCTAD with respect to the economic, commercial and development aspects of the international patent system in the context of its ongoing revision.

The Manila proposals included also a comprehensive programme dealing with the least developed among developing countries, the developing island countries and the developing land-locked countries. These required special measures to help overcome handicaps imposed by history or by geographical isolation. Measures to encourage economic co-operation among developing countries and to increase their "collective self reliance"—a concept born and enlarged upon within UNCTAD—were also contained in the Manila document. Finally there were proposals to increase trade between countries having different economic and social systems and for reviewing the institutional arrangements in UNCTAD in order to enable it to play a decisive role in the further elaboration and implementation of the New International Economic Order.

THE NEGOTIATIONS

The negotiations at UNCTAD IV were of a kind not often seen in the past. They took place as much within the different political groupings as they did among them. Group B, that is the developed market economy countries, in particular was so divided that negotiation with other groups was impossible during most of the conference on most of the issues. Some members of the group, like the Netherlands and Norway, had announced their support for the Manila proposals on commodities even before the conference began.   Others like the Federal Republic of Germany and Japan did not support the integrated programme. The Federal Republic of Germany was opposed to the very concept, while Japan declared a willingness to "exchange views". The United States made no direct reference to the Manila proposals but put forward the idea of an international Resources Bank that would mobilize capital for investment in the production of commodities. The French position seemed comparatively closer to the 77 in so far as the French Finance Minister Jean Pierre Foucarde said "it is quite possible that after a while the creation of a Central Fund may reveal itself as convenient". He suggested that decisions on the nature of the Fund be postponed till a number of commodity arrangements had been signed.

On the question of debt the positions of developed countries again were different. The Scandinavian countries were more supportive of the 77 position, though with some reservations concerning commercial debts. Most other developed countries were opposed to any attempts at looking at all debt problems in a comprehensive manner. As in the case of commodities they preferred here too a case by case approach. On all these matters the position of socialist countries remained the same: the economic condition of the developing countries was not of their making and they did not play any part in perpetuating the existing order. They pointed to bilateral links with developing countries and the healthy growth of such links during the past decade. On the demands in the Manila Declaration that trade between socialist countries and developing countries "should be covered by appropriate payments arrangements, including where required, provisions for the convertibility of surplus balances of developing countries into convertible currencies", there was no positive response.

Facing this array of positions the developing countries showed, for the first time, a cohesiveness that went beyond the general. Commenting on this UNCTAD Secretary General Gamani Corea pointed to the political significance for future negotiations. Not only did the Group of 77 adopt a unified negotiating position on a number of specific concrete issues, he said, they were able in doing so to reconcile the inevitable divergences that might have been expected to exist amongst themselves. "What is more, the Group of 77 showed a capacity not only to maintain a united front in presenting their demands, but also to back up their demands with a willingness to commit their own resources towards the achievement of some of the major objectives they had in mind." This was underlined, he said, by the pledges of support, often in specific financial terms, made by one developing country after another—including OPEC members—for the common fund for commodities.

THE RESULTS

Till the very end of the conference there was no perceptible movement on the main issues. Then, with the scheduled end already past, the negotiations went into overdrive and from a final tumultuous night of meetings there emerged 12 consensus resolutions. The ink was not yet dry on them when the questions were already being asked about their significance. Would they affect the way the world ordered its trade; would they affect patterns of development?

The answer varies with the point of view and the yardstick used to measure success. As Gamani Corea told the Economic and Social Council a month after the conference, "one can evaluate the results of Nairobi on the basis of the Manila Declaration and Programme of Action of the Group of 77. One can judge the results in terms of the positions taken by the developed countries prior to Nairobi, although these were not embodied in a single formulation. One can assess the outcome of the conference in terms of the proposals made by the UNCTAD secretariat itself, which were not identical to those made in the Manila document. Again, one can compare the results with one's prior expectations of what was possible, taking account of all the forces at work at the conference."

"I believe myself", Mr. Corea went on, "that useful as assessments by these several yardsticks might be, the essential criterion by which to judge the usefulness of UNCTAD IV is whether and to what extent it has made a difference to the prospects for international economic relations which prevailed prior to the conference. Has UNCTAD IV brought us to a new stage from which we can proceed, or has it left us very much where we were before the conference?

Answering his own question, Mr. Corea pointed to what he considered significant progress in some areas, and the lack of any in others. On commodities, he said, there was "by consensus, an endorsement of the Integrated Programme for Commodities, including the objectives and mechanisms that are an essential part of that programme. In the provisions of the resolution...there are many innovations and many advances that have not been previously recorded in any decision by the international community on the commodity issue...a new framework has been established within which the problem can be dealt with in the future. I see this as a major step forward".

On the "major problem of the external debt of developing countries" Mr. Corea said he was "quite frankly...disappointed" by the conference resolution. It "did not embody any specific commitment regarding the action to be taken to relieve the immediate debt problems of the developing countries. What it did contain was a commitment on the part of the creditor countries to respond quickly and constructively, with a sense of urgency, to individual requests for debt relief...and it now remains to be seen to what extent this commitment is acted upon..." But it could not be said that there was no movement at all on debt, he added. It had been agreed that existing international fora would work at identifying common elements in dealing with individual cases of debt relief, and this could be seen as a beginning towards establishing guidelines for general policies in the field. Moreover, it had been decided that the Trade and Development Board, expanded to the full membership of UNCTAD and meeting at the ministerial level in 1977, would review action, both in specific cases of debt relief and in building up a framework for policy.

In the area of trade in manufactures and semi-manufactures, Mr. Corea said that the resolution spelt out "a set of inter-related and mutually supporting measures" to deal with the problems of developing countries. While the comprehensive programme that had been asked for did not materialize, the resolution did allow, along with the resolution relating to transnational corporations, a "considerable basis on which to build in the future". In the realm of transfer of technology UNCTAD IV had been "particularly successful" he said. It set the stage for work on the drafting and adopting of a code of conduct on the transfer of technology; it recognized the prominent role of UNCTAD in the ongoing work of revision of the industrial property system; and most importantly it had given new emphasis to the building up of the technological capability of developing countries. To help in this latter process a new national and international institutional framework was envisaged, and UNCTAD was called upon to provide an advisory service to developing countries.

Besides the significant advances on specific items, the main result of UNCTAD IV is that negotiations will continue (See annex for schedule of talks). They will continue on the question of setting up a common fund to finance international and national buffer stocks of commodities. They will continue on setting up regional and inter-regional centres of technology. They will continue on drawing up a draft code of conduct on the transfer of technology. They will continue on the question of convertibility of currencies of the socialist states in their trade relations with developing countries. The developing countries themselves will continue to negotiate, seeking greater "collective self-reliance". UNCTAD will continue its watching brief over the negotiations under GATT. It will convene its next conference within the next three (instead of four) years and before then its Trade and Development Board, with its new open-ended membership, will meet once at the ministerial level. There are specific time-tables for agreement on a variety of subjects and if they are observed the world will indeed have been moved by the resolutions taken at UNCTAD IV. [The timetable for negotiations under UNCTAD auspices is given in Annex I]

CHAPTER V

THE PARIS TALKS

The Paris Talks—as the Conference on International Economic Co-operation is familiarly known—grew out of a proposal that the President of France first made during a press conference on 24 October 1974. What he proposed then was a meeting to focus on the problems of energy supply and price, but at the insistence of developing countries and after protracted negotiations the subject of the talks was widened to include the problems of raw materials, money and finance, and of development as a whole.

Of the 27 countries participating in the conference, 19 represent the Group of 77 (developing countries) and 8 represent developed countries with market economies. Both groups were chosen by and represent their larger camps and maintain close liaison with them. The representatives of developing countries are Algeria, Argentina, Brazil, Cameroon, Egypt, India, Indonesia, Iran, Iraq, Jamaica, Mexico, Nigeria, Pakistan, Peru, Saudi Arabia, Venezuela, Yugoslavia, Zaire and Zambia. The developed countries are represented by Australia, Canada, Japan, Spain, Sweden, Switzerland and the United States, as well as by a joint delegation of the European Economic Community.

At the first meeting of the conference in Paris in December 1975 the attending ministers decided to establish four Commissions: on Energy, Raw Materials, Development, and on Financial Affairs. Each Commission consists of 15 members, 10 from developing countries and five from developed countries. It was agreed that the Commissions would meet periodically throughout 1976 and present their conclusions to another ministerial meeting to be convened a year from the first meeting.

The Paris talks are not under United Nations auspices but there are close ties with the world body. Not only is the United Nations secretariat invited to attend as a permanent observer, but so are a number of other bodies within the United Nations system (UNCTAD, FAO, UNDP, UNIDO, IBRD, IMF). The role of United Nations observers has varied from one Commission to the other. They have been called upon to provide some Commissions with substantive support which the purely technical conference secretariat cannot do. At the first ministerial session of the talks, explicit note was taken of the resolution adopted by the Seventh Special Session of the United Nations General Assembly, and it was agreed that a report would be made to the thirty-first session of the Assembly in 1976.

All this, as United Nations Secretary-General Kurt Waldheim observed at the first session of the talks, was only appropriate: "In deciding that the United Nations would be associated with this conference a welcome sensitivity has been shown to the requirements of continuity and the need for coherence in a multiple negotiation. The United Nations has been the melting pot where the political impulse needed for this event was shaped. It has prepared the minds, stirred the consciences and developed the competence and experience—all elements essential in the maturation of new ideas." The Paris talks, the Secretary-General went on, "should be seen as an integral part of a broader process of negotiation toward the re-ordering of the world's priorities..."

Courtesy Jean Plantureux

In July a meeting of senior officials marked the conclusion of the first phase of the talks. They issued a communique which said in part that the "senior officials agreed that the CIEC had completed the initial phase of its work, in which analytical discussions were held on a wide range of international economic problems of concern to both developing and industrialized countries. While there was some recognition that the analytical work had contributed to a greater understanding of the problems under consideration at the Conference, some disappointment was expressed at the lack of concrete results during the first phase of the Conference". The "disappointment" was stressed in the speeches of most representatives of developing countries; they felt that there had been little progress during the first six months of the talks.

The senior officials also agreed that the second phase of the talks would be "action oriented". They directed the Commissions to "concentrate their work on formulating concrete proposals for action to be submitted to the Ministerial Conference for adoption . . ." The concluding ministerial conference of the series is to be held in mid-December 1976. Before then the Commissions will have met four times (in July, September, October and November). The July meeting was supposed to have finalized the work programme for the rest of the year but did not do so.

The talks resumed in September on the basis of a programme agreed upon by the two co-chairmen of the conference, but little progress was made by the end of 1976 when the talks were to conclude. It was agreed to continue the dialogue into 1977. Meanwhile, the U.N. General Assembly meeting in New York adopted a resolution in December 1976, expresssing "its deep concern and disappointment at the failure of the CIEC to achieve any concrete results so far, and its profound concern at the adverse effect which the failure of the conference will have on international economic co-operation". It urged the "developed countries participating in the conference to respond positively to the proposals put forward by the developing countries . . .".

In January 1977 Robert McNamara, President of the World Bank, proposed that a group of eminent persons from developing and developed countries be assembled to try in their personal capacities to evolve means to break the deadlock in negotiations, The U.N. Secretary General supported the proposal but Manuel Perez Guerrero of Venezuela, one of the two Co-Chairmen of the Paris Talks, issued a statement expressing his "misgivings". The talks in Paris, he said, could succeed if governments strengthened their will to agree. Such success would have positive effects on other negotiations within the United Nations.

The members of the four Commissions at the talks are as follows (the co-chairmen of each body are italicized):

ENERGY: Algeria, Brazil, Canada, Egypt, EEC, India, Iran, Iraq, Jamaica, Japan, *Saudi Arabia*, Switzerland, *United States*, Venezuela and Zaire.

RAW MATERIALS: Argentina, Australia, Cameroon, EEC, Indonesia, *Japan*, Mexico, Nigeria, *Peru*, Spain, United States, Venezuela, Yugoslavia, Zaire, Zambia.

DEVELOPMENT: *Algeria*, Argentina, Cameroon, Canada, *EEC*, India, Jamaica, Japan, Nigeria, Pakistan, Peru, Sweden, United States, Yugoslavia, Zaire.

FINANCE: Brazil, *EEC*, Egypt, India, Indonesia, *Iran*, Iraq, Japan, Mexico, Pakistan, Saudi Arabia, Sweden, Switzerland, United States, Zambia.

CHAPTER VI

THE GATT MULTILATERAL TRADE NEGOTIATIONS

The post-war period, up to the middle of 1973, was a period of unprecedented economic expansion in the developed countries. A contributing factor in this expansion was the progressive dismantling of barriers to the free flow of trade among these countries. Reductions in tariff barriers were negotiated in successive "rounds" under the auspices of the General Agreement on Tariffs and Trade (GATT). Major quantitative restrictions of developed market economy countries were reduced or eliminated in the early post-war period under the aegis of the Organization for Economic Co-operation and Development (OECD), although a number of restrictions remained. But on the whole, relatively little progress was made in reducing barriers on products of particular export interest to developing countries.

The GATT was based on the premise that trade liberalization and reliance on market forces would bring about an adequate distribution of the benefits of economic growth. However, the normal operation of market forces has not resulted in the majority of developing countries enjoying export earnings which are adequate and reasonably stable in real terms to support their development programmes. Even in the period of rapid economic expansion, relatively few developing countries gained any substantial benefits from world economic growth. During the present international economic crisis, there has been a general decline in the prices of the major commodity exports of developing countries other than oil, while continuing inflation in the developed market economy countries has resulted in continuing and substantial increases in the prices of their exports to developing countries.

THE MULTILATERAL TRADE NEGOTIATIONS

The multilateral trade negotiations were formally launched by a Declaration adopted on 14 September 1973 by the representatives of 102 countries at a Ministerial Meeting in Tokyo.* That Declaration identified as the general objectives of the negotiations the expansion and further liberalization of world trade and the securing of additional benefits for the trade of developing countries. It states that the negotiations would cover tariff and non-tariff barriers to trade in agricultural and industrial products. It also set out the guiding principles for the conduct of the negotiations, namely mutual advantage, mutual commitment, over-all reciprocity, and application of the most-favoured-nation clause. However, it recognized that special measures needed to be taken to assist the developing countries, especially the least developed among them, and that differential measures should be applied to developing countries in a way which would provide for special and more favourable treatment for them where feasible and appropriate. The importance of maintaining and improving the generalized system of preferences was also recognized.

The negotiations were activated in 1975 after the enactment of legislation** in the United States of America enabling that country's administration to participate in the negotiations. Until then, the Trade Negotiations Committee established by the Tokyo Ministerial Meeting had not been able to progress beyond consideration of the modalities of the negotiations. It was the fourth session of the Committee, in February 1975, which marked the beginning of the actual negotiating process.

At that session, the Committee established six specialized working groups, each of which is to lay the ground for detailed negotiations in its area of responsibility. The terms of reference of these working groups correspond to six specific negotiating aims set out in paragraph 3 of the Tokyo Declaration, namely:

---

*By the terms of the Declaration, the negotiations are open to any Government which notifies the Director-General of GATT of its intention to participate. So far, 23 Governments not members of GATT have made such notifications, while 29 Governments members of GATT or *de facto* adherents are not participating in the negotiations. Thus, while the multilateral trade negotiations are serviced by GATT secretariat, use GATT facilities and follow GATT practices, participation in them differs substantially from the membership of GATT itself.

**The United States Trade Reform Act of 1974, which became law on 3 January 1975.

"(a)   To conduct negotiations on *tariffs* by employment of appropriate formulae of as general application as possible;

"(b)   To reduce or eliminate *non-tariff* measures or, where this is not
appropriate, to reduce or eliminate their trade restricting or dis-
torting effects, and to bring such measures under more effective
international discipline;

"(c)   To include an examination of the possibilities for the co-ordinated reduction or elimination of all barriers to trade in selected
sectors as a complementary technique;

"(d)   To include an examination of the adequacy of the multilateral
safeguard system, considering particularly the modalities of
application of Article XIX of the GATT, with a view to furthering trade liberalization and preserving its results;

"(e)   To include, as regards *agriculture*, an approach to negotiations
which, while in line with the general objectives of the negotiations, should take account of the special characteristics and problems in this sector;

"(f)   To treat tropical products as a special and priority sector."

The multilateral trade negotiations have thus been initiated in these
areas. It should be noted, however, that several Governments or developed countries have indicated their desire to include in the negotiations
the issue of access to supplies of food-stuffs, fuels and industrial raw
materials—an issue which came to the fore after the adoption of the
Tokyo Declaration. References have been made in some recent working
group meetings to possible ways of doing this. Group meetings started in
March 1975. The Trade Negotiations Committee is to review the progress of the work of the groups. The following is a brief summary of
their work:

(a)   The *Group on Tariffs* is undertaking to draw up a tariff negotiating plan of as general application as possible, taking into account the
importance of maintaining and improving the general system of preferences. Discussions have been primarily on technical considerations but it
is expected that tariff negotiations will intensify in the autumn when
United States negotiators will have the authority to make concrete proposals;

(b)   The *Group on Non-Tariff Measures* was able to reach agreement
on a list of specific issues on which negotiations could be initiated, on the

understanding that other measures might be added at a later date and that no non-tariff measure was being excluded from the negotiations;

(c)   The *Group on the Sector Approach* agreed that due account would be taken in its work of the specific trade problems of developing countries and of the need to apply differential measures in ways which would provide special and more favourable treatment for developing countries. The GATT secretariat was asked to collect trade data in the ores and metals sector. It is also examining various negotiating problems and the impact of the sector approach on the trade of the developing countries;

(d)   The *Group on Safeguards* decided to conduct an examination of the operation of the present multilateral safeguard system and, if this revealed inadequacies, to carry out an examination of the elements that should be built into a new or revised system, bearing in mind in particular the special interests of the developing countries, which are seeking differential treatment for their trade;

(e)   The *Group on Agriculture* was unable to reach agreement on the organization of the negotiations or agricultural products, owing to a difference of views between the European Economic Community and the United States of America. Discussions between these two parties are to continue with the objective of finding a mutually acceptable compromise which will make it possible to start substantive negotiations in this area;

(f)   The *Group on Tropical Products* agreed that, given the special priority of this area, substantive negotiations should be undertaken as soon as possible. It was decided that exporting countries, individually or in groups, should submit specific request lists to the major market countries, identifying the concessions they wished to obtain from them. These requests would be circulated multilaterally and then the question of offers would be discussed.

In late 1976 the first results from the negotiations were announced. They related to the demands some 44 developing countries had made to 11 developed countries for tariff and non-tariff concessions covering tropical products which are important export items for developing countries.

In December 1976 Australia, the European Economic Community, Finland, Norway, Sweden, New Zealand and Switzerland announced that some concessions would be in effect from 1 January 1977. It is expected that Austria, Canada and Japan will put their concessions into effect in the foreseeable future as soon as necessary domestic procedures have been completed.

CONSIDERATION OF NEW PRINCIPLES AND RULES FOR THE CONDUCT OF INTERNATIONAL TRADE

The Tokyo Declaration reaffirmed support for the principles, rules and disciplines of the GATT (though it was noted that this reaffirmation did not necessarily represent the views of countries not then parties to the General Agreement). It went on to state that "consideration shall be given to improvements in the international framework for the conduct of world trade which might be desirable in the light of progress in the negotiations and, in this endeavour, care shall be taken to ensure that any measures introduced as a result are consistent with the over-all objectives and principles of the trade negotiations and particularly of trade liberalization".

In the course of the multilateral trade negotiations, a number of articles of the GATT will come under examination and be the subject of proposed amendments. Among the articles which have already been mentioned in this context are those relating to quantitative controls, licensing, emergency action on imports of particular products (safeguards), subsidies, anti-dumping and countervailing duties, valuation for customs purposes, and consular formalities. It has been suggested that their reform may consist in amending the articles in question or may be achieved through the formulation of guidelines or legally binding codes. The developing countries have generally aimed at incorporating in the provisions of the GATT, wherever appropriate, an element of preferential or special treatment for their trade. It is not clear at this stage how far and how comprehensively the reform of the GATT will be carried out as part of the negotiations—and, in particular, to what extent the kind of changes contemplated would alter the economic relationships between developed and developing countries.

The consideration of new principles and rules for the conduct of international trade raises fundamental questions of a substantive and an institutional character which have a bearing upon the structure of the United Nations system in the area of development and international economic co-operation. It is in this connexion that a call has been made for the establishment of a "comprehensive international trade organization".

CHAPTER VII

COMMISSION ON TRANSNATIONAL CORPORATIONS

If the growth in number of nation-states is the most remarkable political phenomenon of the post-war world, the most significant economic development is that of the transnational corporation. In size and geographical reach, in the multiplicity of activities, in the command of resources and of power many corporations now rival nations. This has naturally made transnational corporations a subject of deep interest at the international level. They have been depicted in some quarters as key instruments for maximizing world welfare, and in some others as subversive to the sover-

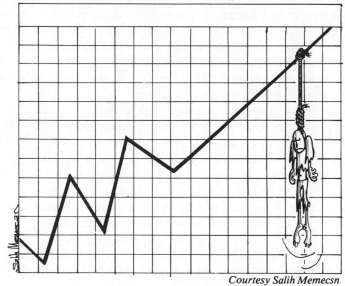

Courtesy Salih Memecsn

39

eignty of peoples. The basic facts and issues, however, still need to be studied and analyzed, and to this end the United Nations Economic and Social Council set up a 48-member Commission and a Centre on Transnational Corporations.

At the first meeting of the Commission in March 1975 a programme of work was established for the Centre, a unit directly attached to the Office of the United Nations Secretary-General. The work set out was geared to three objectives. First, to further the understanding of the nature and the political, legal, economic and social effects of the activities of transnational corporations. Second, to secure effective international arrangements for the operations of transnational corporations. And finally, to strengthen the negotiating capacity of host developing countries in their dealing with the corporations.

At the second meeting of the Commission in March 1976 in Lima, Peru, the Commission laid the foundations upon which the future work of the United Nations would be built. "The decisions taken at Lima, and equally important, the spirit in which they were taken" says Klaus Sahlgren, Executive Director of the Centre on Transnationals, "provide important indicators of the progress that can be expected during the next few years." The session was characterized by a determined effort by all Governments to avoid confrontation and to make progress on the basis of full consensus. While many of the differences that have manifested themselves in the past still exist, all members of the Commission recognized the necessity not to get bogged down in them. Full and unanimous agreement was reached on the initial areas of attention and on the modalities that should be followed to achieve them.

The Commission's most important decision was on the issue of a code of conduct, to which it clearly assigned the highest priority. Although disagreements continue on such key questions as whether the code of conduct should be compulsory, voluntary, or voluntary with some machinery for the surveillance of its application, the Governments gathered in Lima did agree that any code that was adopted should be effective. They also agreed that on the time-table for preparing the code and on the procedures to be followed. Briefly, the details are as follows: a working group representing all members of the Commission has been established, to meet during the next two years. It has been asked to submit an annotated outline of the code of conduct to the third session of the Commission in the spring of 1977. On the basis of further instructions then, the working group will prepare the full text of the code and submit it in the spring of 1978.

The working group has been requested to carry out its task on the basis of a number of inputs; namely, the proposals and views on the code which will emerge from meetings of Governments at the regional levels, as well as proposals and views received from individual Governments. In addition, non-governmental interests, particularly trade unions, business and consumer groups will also be invited to submit their views. Finally, the Centre has been requested to prepare two documents. First an action-oriented paper covering all the issues involved, and a second paper dealing with the possible structural alternatives of a code of conduct and their implications. The working group will start its work early in 1977.

When establishing the Commission, the Economic and Social Council called upon it to select persons with extensive practical experience in trade unions, business and public interest groups, and to associate them in its work. The Commission was unable to take a decision on this matter at its first session, but at the same session it requested the Secretary-General, in consultation with all members of the Commission, to propose 12 to 15 persons with extensive practical experience in trade unions, business, consumer groups and other public interest groups. These persons would thus be available for consultations to the working group and to the fourth session of the Commission.

IMPORTANCE OF OTHER AREAS RECOGNIZED

While stressing that the formulation of a code of conduct received the highest priority, the Commission recognized the importance of moving ahead concurrently in a number of other areas. The Commission requested the Centre to move ahead speedily with the collection of publicly available information of a general or specific nature, including the preparation of profiles on individual transnational corporations, as well as the collection of data on contracts and agreements between transnational corporations and government agencies or national enterprises. The Commission recognized the magnitude of this task and urged that the necessary computer facilities be made available to the Centre. Without wishing to minimize the importance of publicly available information the Commission was aware of the constraints resulting from existing national legislation or from the requirement of business confidentiality which may present obstacles to the collection of information which is normally not publicly available. It requested the Centre to undertake a feasibility study in order to identify more clearly what the problems are and what measures could be considered to overcome them. The Commission also stressed the importance of moving ahead speedily with the establishment of standards for developing and collecting comparable information.

PROBLEM-ORIENTED RESEARCH

In the area of research, the Commission concluded from the survey carried out by the Centre that while considerable work is being done it is not sufficiently problem-oriented and does not focus adequately on the impact of transnational corporations on developing countries. The Commission therefore decided on a considerable amount of work to be carried out or promoted by the Centre ranging from a comprehensive integrated study which will be a sequel to the study carried out in 1973, to in-depth studies covering such vital issues as the impact of transnational corporations on the balance of payments of developing countries, the effects of investments by transnational corporations on investment and production by domestic enterprises, the effects of transnational corporations on employment as well as the role of transnational corporations in banking, insurance, shipping, tourism, the extractive food and pharmaceutical industries.

Finally, the Commission attached great importance to the Centre's technical co-operation programme which is aimed at strengthening the negotiating capacity of the developing countries.

ACTION ON CORRUPT PRACTICES

In addition to the General Assembly requesting the Centre to undertake studies on corrupt practices of transnational corporations, the Commission had before it a proposal by the United States which called for the establishment of a working group to prepare an international agreement on this subject. This initiative was generally appreciated and welcomed. However, most delegations felt that more time was needed to study this proposal as well as any other possible approach.

"A good deal was accomplished in Lima", Mr. Klaus Sahlgren told reporters after the conclusion of the session. "Of course many serious problems remain to be resolved but an important process has been launched under very promising conditions. Much work, debate and negotiations still need to take place. The Commission's functions over the next few years will be of great importance."

CHAPTER VIII

FOOD

Rome was the venue for two major meetings on issues related to food in 1976. The first was the United Nations Conference on the Establishment of an International Fund for Agricultural Development (IFAD). The second was the meeting of the World Food Council. Both meetings were part of the same process: the implementation of the resolutions of the World Food Conference, also held in Rome, in 1974.

The 1974 World Food Conference had pin-pointed a crucial element in economic development: the urgent need to increase the growth rate of food production in the developing world. United Nations economists had estimated that to feed the world's growing population, food production should grow by 4 per cent annually in developing countries during the Second United Nations Development Decade (1970-80). But by the middle of the Decade an increase of only 2.4 per cent a year was being achieved. If this rate could not be stepped up the developing world faced the prospect of a cereals deficit of from 85 to 100 million tons by 1985.

The proposal to set up an International Fund for Agricultural Development was adopted by the World Food Conference in Rome in 1974. Sponsored by 34 nations, including 11 members of the Organization of Petroleum Exporting Countries (OPEC), 19 other developing countries and three developed nations, the resolution called on the Secretary-General of the United Nations to urgently convene a meeting of interested countries to work out details of the Fund. The Secretary-General charged the Executive Director of the World Food Council, Dr. John A. Hannah, with the task of organizing the negotiations. The 36 member Council, the highest international political body dealing with food, had been created by the United Nations General Assembly to follow-up the

44

World Food Conference's resolutions and sharpen the international community's political response to world food problems.

GRAIN-FOR THE RICH WORLD'S ANIMALS OR THE POOR WORLD'S PEOPLE ?
Courtesy ACB

CONCEPT OF FUND

Three meetings of interested countries—in Geneva in May 1975, in Rome in October 1975 and in February 1976—worked out details of a draft agreement for the Fund. It is conceived of as a *development* fund which will disburse grants and loans on highly concessional terms to increase food production in the developing world. The organizational structure of the Fund will be innovative, with the votes shared equally by three categories of countries: developing donor (OPEC) nations; developing recipient countries; and developed countries. Thus two-thirds of the votes lie with developing countries, who will therefore have a major influence on the investment decisions of the Fund, and at the same time two-thirds of the votes are held by donor countries.

The resolution of the World Food Conference proposing IFAD stipulated that disbursements from the Fund should be carried out through existing international and regional institutions. The Fund will thus be able to keep its central administration small, by operating through existing organizations such as the World Bank, the Food and Agricultural Organization of the United Nations (FAO), regional Development Banks, and the United Nations Development Programme (UNDP), but it will set the priorities for project selection and retain ultimate control over its projects. The Fund will disburse its resources partly through grants and mainly in the form of concessional loans. It will also be able to undertake joint financing with other regional or national funds or with private financing and agro-business organizations.

According to the Agreement on IFAD negotiated in Rome in 1976, the target for initial funding was $1,000 million in convertible currencies. This target was passed in December 1976 and the U.N. Secretary-General declared the IFAD Agreement open for signature. In doing so he pointed to the significance not only of increasing the resources committed to agricultural development, but of the nature of the new partnership of the countries involved. "The establishment of IFAD is integral to the effort now underway to build a new international economic order," he said. "It demonstrates that with the necessary political will, the elements of a new order can be designed, negotiated and put into place."

THE WORLD FOOD COUNCIL

Immediately following the meeting to set up IFAD, the World Food Council met for its second ministerial session in Rome. The 36-nation Council had been established at the Ministerial level by the General Assembly to give political impetus to the world food strategy adopted by the 1974 World Food Conference. The secretariat of the Council had been responsible for the negotiations to set up IFAD and the ministerial session now turned to three other key factors in the world situation: food security, food aid and increasing food production in developing countries.

These issues had been thrust into the international arena during the world food crisis of 1972 to 1974. Poor harvests in many parts of the world had led to a sharp drop in world grain reserves and alarming increases in prices which affected all countries, rich and poor. The 1974 World Food Conference had thus called for international action to ensure that food grains were available during bad harvest years and to stabilize prices. With agreement reached in principle that action was needed, discussions on the subject have ranged in the last two years from meetings of the General Agreement on Tariffs and Trade, to the International Wheat Council, the FAO and UNCTAD.

The Food Council session this year established that progress is being made on several aspects of the problem. Firstly, a number of developed nations are already taking practical steps towards putting aside emergency stocks of grain for a 500,000 ton international stockpile to ensure that food is available to be rushed to countries hit by droughts, floods, earthquakes and other natural disasters. In addition, the European Economic Community and other nations including Canada, a major wheat producer, have committed themselves to ensuring that their food aid commitments are made on the basis of a three-year planning period. Progress on this issue is a step towards guaranteeing that even in bad years, the annual target of 10 million tons of food aid would be available.

The larger question of food security to stabilize prices is an extremely complex one, involving as it does a major and highly political aspect of world trade. Again, most nations have accepted in principle that the international community must take action, but negotiations have not so far solved the problems of the decision-making mechanisms and criteria upon which a 15 to 20 million ton reserve of grain would be established and managed to act as an insurance mechanism to prevent extreme fluctuations in prices. The Group of 77 made clear at the Council that they regard such a food security system as a vital component in a new international economic order, but the major producing and exporting nations, and the developed consumer nations have not yet been able to agree on the technical arrangements that will be needed to put a food security system into action.

The Council did agree, however, on the need to establish a new category of nations, to be known as "food priority nations". The criteria for inclusion in this category include good potential for increasing food production, low nutrition levels, dependence on imports, and an unsatisfactory historical increase in food production. Acceptance of this new category of about 40 nations will help focus and make more efficient multilateral and bilateral assistance for increasing food production in the developing world and ensure that aid will be concentrated on the nations which will most benefit from it.

CHAPTER IX

THE WORLD EMPLOYMENT CONFERENCE

Unique among the recent series of international meetings was the World Employment Conference in Geneva (4 to 17 June 1976). Held under the auspices of the International Labour Organisation (ILO), it brought together some 1,300 representatives of three different groups: governments, workers and employers. They came from 121 countries to discuss a basic problem of development: the use of human resources during a period of rapid population growth and social change.

The years since the Second World War have been, in many respects, a period of unprecedented social and economic progress. The world economy and trade have expanded at rates which have no parallel in recorded history. The developed countries, both with market economies and central planning, have enjoyed ever-rising levels of prosperity and affluence. Taken as a whole, the developing countries, many of which embarked upon systematic planning to accelerate development in the fifties and sixties, have succeeded in attaining aggregate rates of economic growth which are impressive by the standards of the past.

Yet the very pace and pattern of world development over the past quarter of a century have generated profound social, economic and ecological imbalances—to the extent that doubts are now being cast on the continuing validity of past patterns of development. The fruits of economic growth and of the benefits flowing from the international economic system have been unevenly distributed. Many developing countries have made little progress and even those that have are nowhere near raising the mass of their people to an adequate standard of living.

Despite all efforts, the numbers of illiterates and those without adequate shelter show no sign of decline. Unemployment has reached crisis

49

proportions in a large number of countries. In quantitative terms, the problems of under-employment and inadequate incomes are even more serious. The benefits of economic growth in many countries have been concentrated among a small minority of the population. Thus the structures of income and wealth distribution are marked by sharp and, in some cases, by growing inequalities.

The developed countries have their own problems of poverty, unemployment and income disparities, though they are on a vastly different scale from those experienced by the developing countries. The rate and pattern of growth experienced by them have created another set of problems—of ecological imbalances, environmental degradation and social stress. Some of the developed market economies have fuelled their economic growth by the massive importation of labour, and have only more recently come to consider the longer-term implications of their policies with regard to foreign workers. In some countries, inflation and scarcity of vital natural resources and raw materials are perceived as constituting a grave threat to growth and welfare.

The Employment Conference approached this range of problems from a position of unique vantage. Its tripartite structure—with representatives of governments, workers and employers sitting together—gave it the ability to study and act in a manner more comprehensive than other meetings. The Conference had a five-point agenda that focussed attention on issues related to employment strategies, international migration of workers, technology, transnational enterprises, and the need to assist the process of international change. The outcome of the meeting took the form of a Declaration of Principles and a Programme of Action, adopted without dissent but after long and often contentious deliberation.

The delegates were in agreement that satisfying the basic needs of the world's poorest people should be the priority objective of development during the next 25 years. At the same time the Conference declared that changes in the international economic order should not be made at the expense of any workers. Developed countries were urged to achieve and maintain full employment, and also to take special measures to ensure equal treatment for women, migrants, the young and the handicapped.

To provide the basic amenities of life to the least privileged sections of the world's people, the meeting called for the accelerated increase in

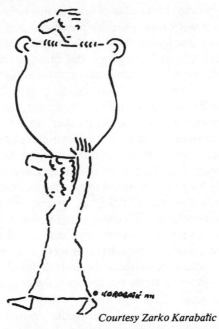

Courtesy Zarko Karabatic

production and in the creation of new jobs. The targets set for the current Second Development Decade should be revised with the aim of providing for the basic needs of the most deprived people, the Conference urged. And the Third Development Decade should be planned with the same "basic needs programme" as its core. To this end it was recommended that part of the $1,000 million International Fund for Agricultural Development (see Chapter VIII) should be earmarked for the creation of employment in rural sectors of developing countries. The Conference also called for action to prevent the exploitation of migrant labour and to limit the harmful effects of migration on people and on their countries. The development of technologies best suited to the resources and potential of developing countries was also urged.

The Conference called upon the ILO to set up a world-wide programme of household surveys to map the nature, extent and causes of poverty. This would help countries to establish the statistical and monitoring services necessary to formulate basic needs policies and to measure progress toward their achievement. The ILO was asked to report on basic needs policies to an annual conference before the end of the 1970s, based on information supplied by member states. The organization was also asked to make its technical services available to member countries in choosing appropriate technology and in adjusting to migration trends.

During discussions the participants differed on such matters as the role of transnational companies, population policies, the matching of basic needs to high rates of growth and investment, and adjustments in industrialized countries that would jeopardize employment. The most extensively debated issue was that of transnational companies and their role in development. Government spokesmen from developing countries expressed the view that transnational enterprises contributed to global economic imbalances by their often restrictive business practices (such as the operation of monopolies, fixing of prices, etc.). The sovereignty of developing countries was seen to be threatened by these operations and a strengthening of national institutions was urged as a remedial measure. Regional and international measures were also recommended to ensure that transnationals re-oriented their policies in developing countries.

Government spokesmen for the socialist countries of Eastern Europe supported in principle the position of the developing countries. They felt that transnational corporations should contribute to the creation of employment in their host countries, without hindering either a just distribution of income or social progress. Most government representatives of industrialized market economies underlined the positive effects of the activities of transnationals. Countries which welcomed foreign investment were urged to create a favourable climate for investment so as to encourage companies to adapt their activities to the economic needs of their hosts. They pointed out that the role of transnationals differed from country to country and that their ability to create employment also differed.

The views of Employers and Workers tended in the main to follow those of their governments, though they were by no means identical. The representatives of Employers from developed market economies stressed the importance of transnational corporations as vehicles for the transfer of technology and of managerial skills. The choice of technology was often dictated by the governments of developing countries, they said, and often there was insistence on the most advanced technology even though it might be unsuitable. Studies by the ILO had shown that the majority of transnationals behaved responsibly, and therefore the Employers from developed countries were unconvinced of the need for international controls. The Employer representatives from the socialist states of Eastern Europe differed in this by fully supporting the views of their government spokesmen and calling for international guidelines and controls.

The representatives of Workers expressed concern at the impact of transnationals on both the availability of jobs and development. They wanted steps at the national and international levels to strengthen control of transnational enterprises. One of the measures proposed would ensure that the profits of a transnational company did not leave its host country. The representatives of Workers recognized the importance of the principle of non discrimination between transnational and national enterprises, but stressed that the very nature of the former made discriminatory measures necessary if developing countries were to protect their own interests. These representatives urged the elaboration of an international code of conduct with binding effect on transnational corporations.

Summing up the results of the Conference, ILO Director General Francis Blanchard pointed to three major points of agreement: (1) The "basic needs strategy" had been unanimously backed, he said, and in future it would be "the touchstone for all development policies". (2) There had been consensus on the interdependent nature of national economies and on the need for concerted international action to promote employment and combat poverty. The policies of industrialized countries could not be determined solely in the interests of those countries, he said. They would have to take into consideration the impact of their policies on the poorest people in developing countries. (3) The Conference had recognized that the reduction of unemployment and the struggle against poverty implied high economic growth rates for developed and developing countries. "This increased growth should come primarily in those areas most suited to the creation of employment and the satisfaction of basic needs", said Mr. Blanchard.

CHAPTER X

HABITAT: THE CONFERENCE ON HUMAN SETTLEMENTS

Before UNCTAD IV had quite ended in Nairobi, and four days before the World Employment Conference met in Geneva, yet another international meeting convened in Vancouver. It was Habitat, the United Nations Conference on Human Settlements. Longer in the planning than most world meetings (it had been conceived at the Stockholm Conference on the Environment in 1972), Habitat brought to fruition two years of complex interdisciplinary study and preparation. It was the first time a global view had been attempted of the ways we live, rich and poor, in city and country, from mountain tops to deserts, from the vast savannas to the seas.

It addressed itself both to the challenge of the future and the pain of the present. In the next 30 years the world's population will double, which means mankind will have to duplicate every building, service, and place of employment if the human family is to live in a condition equal to that of today. And the situation today is far from happy. Towns and cities throughout the world are plagued by shortages of such essentials as food and water. They are beset with problems of unemployment, pollution, congestion, slums and squatter settlements, inadequate transportation, social alienation and crime. During the next 30 years these problems must be dealt with if "development" is to be meaningful. The Habitat Conference sought to underline the recognition that the most pressing problems of human settlements could be solved if the will existed to make the necessary political and social adjustments.

To discuss all this the Vancouver conference brought together high-level government officials and an interesting assortment of others con-

Courtesy Jean Plantureux

cerned with the man-made environment. Leavening the usual diplomatic and political mix were the people who plan our habitat and build them; those who administer and those who study them; and the new breed of those who make it their business to see that in doing all this we do not infringe on the rights of the rest of natural creation. City planners and architects, anthropologists and cybernetists, educators and environmentalists gave Habitat a unique character.

During their two-week meeting these representatives of 131 countries drew up a blueprint for national and international action to improve the living places of people throughout the world. They adopted a Declaration of Principles and a series of recommendations dealing with problems that are now almost universal: housing shortages, the social and economic crises of big cities and rural areas, the proper use of land, the inadequacy of essential services and of popular participation in the solution of problems. Broadly, the Vancouver conference resolutions contain three main elements:

A "Vancouver Declaration on Human Settlements 1976" intended as a broad guide for bettering standards in villages, towns and cities, and starting from the premise that "the improvement of the quality of life of human beings is the first and most important objective of every human settlement policy".

A set of 64 recommendations, addressed directly to Governments, suggesting concrete ways in which people might be assured the basic requirements of human habitation—shelter, clean water, sanitation and a decent physical environment, plus the opportunity for cultural growth and the development of the individual.

A resolution calling for action to set up new United Nations machinery concerned exclusively with human settlements, including an intergovernmental body and a central secretariat whose job would be to help countries to better the lot of their citizens in urban and rural communities everywhere.

Habitat introduced an electronic innovation into the Conference proceedings—the audio-visual "statement". A total of 236 film and slide presentations were prepared by 123 countries and 13 organizations especially for the Conference. Whether the subject was water supply or rural-urban migration, increased pollution or preservation of historic monuments, each film endeavoured to show a solution to that problem.

In the formal sessions—in the plenary and in two of the three committees—three-minute "capsule" versions of the films were shown to illustrate a government's policy or action in the field of human settlements. A special Project Presentation Centre enabled delegates to view their choice of full-length films and seminar rooms were available for discussion. Throughout the Conference a local cable television station devoted six hours a day to Habitat films and they were shown continuously in a public theatre.

At the end of the Conference the delegates unanimously recommended that the General Assembly establish an audio-visual information centre on human settlements, to be located at the University of British Columbia in Vancouver.

The Conference also agreed:

To urge all Governments to support and fully participate in the United Nations Water Conference to be held next March at Mar del Plata, Argentina;

To recommend that the General Assembly request the United Nations Secretary-General to submit a report on "the living conditions of the Palestinian people in the occupied territories".

Parallel with the official Conference, a non-governmental "Habitat Forum" was held at Jericho Beach, a few miles outside the city. Private individuals and a broad cross-section of interested organizations participated in this Forum, discussing the same issues as the main meeting, but with a free-wheeling panache the official delegates could seldom match. Formal lectures, less formalized theatre, music, poetry and dance kept the renovated airplane hangars of Jericho Beach humming with activity. It served to underline in very human terms the very human problems being discussed in Vancouver.

CHAPTER XI

THE STATE OF THE ENVIRONMENT

...A point has been reached in history when we must shape our actions throughout the world with a more prudent care for their environmental consequences. Through ignorance or indifference we can do massive and irreversible harm to the earthly environment on which our life and well being depend.

(The Declaration on the Human Environment Stockholm, 1972)

The United Nations conference on the human environment was the first of the mega conferences of the seventies, one of a series that focussed on global problems looming large in the last quarter of the 20th century. Others on population, food, status of women, industrialization, trade, employment and habitat came later, filling in with unpleasant detail and colour the large biospheric canvas unrolled at Stockholm. The call for a new international economic order too came later, and though it was unforeseen in 1972 it now appears a logical and necessary step in dealing with the problems of the environment.

The reason for this is not difficult to find. As the Executive Director of the United Nations Environment Programme says in the 1976 annual report on the State of the Environment, "At one time the environmental problems debated in international organizations would predominantly have been those recognized by the developed countries—the need to control pollution, the desirability of conserving samples of the ecological and genetic richness and the natural beauty of the earth. Since the United Nations conference on the Human Environment, however, it has been increasingly realized that environmental issues are also of vital concern to developing countries and that over much of the world, the environmental problems are still those associated with poverty—poor housing, bad public health, malnutrition and inadequate employment. These problems can only be solved through development. But that development, producing more food and drawing on the still great resources of the planet, needs to be environmentally wise, and to be based upon thorough evaluation of the potential uses of the different regions of this highly variable earth. Short term solutions may all too easily—as they have in many countries—lead to long term losses which a growing world population cannot afford.'' The present order of the world economy—or more appropriately, the present disorder—is of course not based on a

ONE WORLD

"UGH, HUMANS!"

Courtesy Murray Ball

"thorough evaluation of the potential uses of the different regions of the highly variable earth".

"Scientific study can guide development", the UNEP report says. "It is unlikely to provide a magic formula through which all nations can attain the same standard of living at the same cost in economic or human terms. Because the world is heterogenous, nations will continue to differ in their ways of life and in the ways with which they can maintain the basic standard of living their people demand. The diversity in the world environment has also added to the richness of human experience by evoking differently adapted ways of life in different places, and is likely to continue to be reflected in the detailed pattern of development."

The report points out that there are enough success stories to show that much can be done, in countries with different political and ideological systems, to improve the quality of the environment. "Probably the only pollutions still increasing in the world are those whose hazards to man or other forms of life have not yet been demonstrated," it says. "Science, linked to monitoring, is needed to ensure that new pollutants do not create unrecognized hazards. International schemes to screen such substances before they come into widespread use are a welcome recent development. Science can also guide environmental management by defining potentials for land use under different conditions."

The report calls for "international collaboration, on a scale not seen so far in the history of the world...if mankind is to meet basic human needs and, at the same time to safeguard the environment for future generations." The recent ratification of a number of important global conventions on matters relating to the environment "are an encouraging sign in this respect," it says. "Moreover, the interest Governments have shown in environmental matters, demonstrated by the establishment of national environmental machinery in many countries, is further evidence of concern for environmentally sound development. This is important because some countries, at present using a disproportionate share of the earth's resources, may need to learn to do with less, and use what they consume less wastefully, as part of this process. There is nevertheless still a danger, at both national and international levels, that Governments will use the inadequacies of present knowledge as an excuse for deferring action that can and should be taken now, but which may demand adjustment of cherished policies."

"Without political will, science can do nothing," the report concludes. "The essence of the environmental challenge, therefore is political rather than technical."

When the 50-member Governing Council of the United Nations Environment Programme met in Nairobi in April 1976, one of the topics it discussed was the need for this political will in relating environmental policies to development programmes. It was widely recognized that the inter-relationship was complex, and required elaboration. A number of developing countries warned that while the issues of the environment in the development context were better understood now than a few years ago, there was still a potential conflict between the goals of development and the maintenance of a sound environment. Recent discussions of economic matters within the international community, it was pointed out, had not given adequate consideration to environmental implications. The Governing Council appealed to states to reaffirm their commitment to the integration of environmental considerations in development planning, and it authorized the Executive Director to convene an intergovernmental expert group to consider how this could best be done. It is expected that before the 1977 meeting of the Governing Council, the problems will have been studied in more specific terms.

The 1976 meeting of the Governing Council was the first since Maurice Strong, the first Executive Director of UNEP stepped down. The new Executive Director, Mostafa Kamal Tolba, told the Council in his introductory statement that the organization was "entering a new phase". The three previous sessions of the Governing Council had contributed to the refinement of recommendations made in Stockholm, he said; the fourth session had to take stock of what had been done and look to the future. During the existence of the organization, he said, there had been a growing confidence in its efficacy. Each achievement of UNEP "spreads confidence that environmental problems can be tackled and are soluble, and each such achievement encourages more governments to turn to UNEP for assistance".

In October 1976, reporting to the United Nations General Assembly in New York on the activities of UNEP, Mr. Tolba explained the basic premise of the organization's activities. "UNEP sees its job as to promote alternative patterns of development and life styles in both rich and poor countries...to demonstrate that social and economic objectives, starting with the satisfaction of basic human needs, cannot be attained without proper environmental management". Such management, he went on, "we understand as the management of human activities bearing on the environment in such a way as not to destroy the resource base upon which our development effort rests, not to transgress the limits of biological tolerance which the life supporting systems of the planet dictate".

Proper environmental management, Mr. Tolba said, "cannot be achieved without a concerted effort in what we call supporting measures: environmental education and training, increased public awareness of environmental issues, environmental law, and technical assistance to those who need it". UNEP was involved in all these activities, he said.

"In the field of *environmental education*, we are closely involved with UNESCO in planning for a world conference on the subject next year. As regards *training*, we are developing a number of programmes with UNESCO and others. I must confess that a great deal remains to be done with regard to promoting *public awareness of environmental issues* and to providing information to Governments and others on the work of UNEP, but we have taken some initiatives which will be helpful. With respect to *technical assistance*, UNEP has extended and is continuing to extend what I believe to be valuable services, to a large number of developing countries. In the field of *environmental law*, we are taking steps to gather information on international agreements relating to the environment, to promote such agreements, and to study the legal liability and compensation aspects of pollution. We are continuing our work on the subject of natural resources shared by two or more states with a view to presenting the results to the Governing Council at its next session."

Will the world be able to control pollution during a period of accelerated economic development? Will the expense of such control retard growth? And what are the main constraints to success? There are no certain answers to these questions, but a recent United Nations study tried to provide some by envisaging a world in the year 2000 in which development had occurred and pollution been minimized. The study, conducted by a team of economists headed by Nobel Prize Winner Wassily Leontief, worked back from the model of the successful world, analyzing what would have to be done to achieve it. They concluded that "pollution throughout the world is capable of being kept under control

and the cost of doing this will not seriously hinder economic growth."
They also concluded that in general, the principal limits to growth in the
world economy are "political, social and institutional in character,
rather than physical".

CHAPTER XII

TALKING OF MONEY

It is always difficult to talk of money, for those who have it would rather not, and those without it, can't. But despite this and other difficulties the representatives of 44 nations met in July 1944 at Bretton Woods in the United States to create an international monetary system and a body to oversee its operation, the International Monetary Fund (IMF). They also created the International Bank for Reconstruction and Development (IBRD), more commonly known as the World Bank. As the full name of the World Bank implies, its purpose was to help in the rebuilding of Europe after World War II. The IMF was meant to promote international co-operation on monetary problems by facilitating the balanced growth of world trade, promoting exchange stability, and giving confidence to members by making its resources available to them under adequate safeguards. For three decades the system created at Bretton Woods worked. Under the rules laid down there the world economy expanded spectacularly, the war ravaged countries of western Europe were rebuilt and achieved unprecedented levels of prosperity. A growing number of nations newly emerged from colonial rule were also incorporated into the system during the last 30 years. But the net result of all this was increasing controversy, crisis, and finally the failure of the monetary system.

By the end of the sixties it was evident that powerful new forces were at work in the international monetary system, and that the old rules were incapable of coping. Not only had the world economy become larger and more complex, it had developed several centres of power. Differential rates of inflation and productivity led to large and persistent payments imbalances among industrial countries. The close integration of

"Money! Money! Money! Thats all you ever think about!"
Courtesy Terry Hirst

financial markets made it possible for capital to move in massive amounts across national borders, often sparked by speculative motives, and this aggravated the underlying weakness in the national payments situation. These and other developments, coupled with inadequate national adjustment policies, brought about a succession of currency crises which eventually led to a breakdown of the "par value system" established at Bretton Woods and gave way to a generalized "floating" of major currencies; (i.e., currencies no longer had set official values but were allowed to "float" or find their own values in international currency markets). The need for a basic reform of the International Monetary System was recognized for some time and serious discussions began within the Fund in 1972. Subsequent developments with respect to petroleum and other prices gave new urgency and priorities to the reform discussions.

THE IMF

Attempts at reform have, naturally, focussed upon the operation of the International Monetary Fund. The Fund has two important functions. One is to administer a world currency reserve which member countries can tap if they find themselves in balance-of-payments difficulties. The IMF can be envisaged as a kind of giant counting-house in which the contributions (quotas) of member countries are neatly stacked in tidy rows. If a country's monetary system is in trouble and it has difficulty raising the foreign currencies it needs, its government may apply to the IMF which, in exchange for a deposit of the country's own money, will advance the foreign currencies it needs. The borrowing country has to agree to pay back the currency within a given time. Usually it also has to undertake remedial economic policies to eliminate, or at least reduce, the conditions which caused its problems in the first place.

A second, less-known function of the Fund is to formulate the rules of the monetary game which governments are asked to follow and which once they are accepted, the IMF is called upon to enforce. These rules are embodied in the Fund's Articles of Agreement. First adopted at Bretton Woods, these Articles had been amended only once, in 1969, to establish Special Drawing Rights (SDRs), a new form of reserve asset, also sometimes known as "paper-gold".

On 31 March this year, the Executive Directors of the Fund moved to amend the Articles once again. They sent a series of proposed amendments to the Governors of the Fund who, after voting for them, submitted them to their governments for ratification. In many cases, this requires parliamentary action, and therefore tends to take a year to 18 months. The process is currently underway, and when 60 per cent of the members with 80 per cent of the voting power have signified that they accept the changes, the Articles will stand amended. The changes, while highly technical and often obscurely worded, have a significant impact on monetary, trade and capital flows between nations.

EXCHANGE ARRANGEMENTS OF EACH MEMBER'S CHOICE

The first change in the amended Articles is the flexibility provided to member countries in their exchange rate arrangement. Member countries are free to make such currency arrangements as they wish; i.e., to set rates of exchange, let their value float, either singly or jointly with others, or "peg" them to the rates of the currencies of other countries. In return for this new and relative freedom to manage their currencies freely, governments do however undertake to co-operate with each other and the Fund to promote international stability and to foster orderly world economic and financial conditions. Such co-operation from member countries extends, where necessary, to the internal financial and economic policies which they pursue. This new undertaking would represent an advance for the cause of international co-operation over previous formulations.

THE DIMINISHING ROLE OF GOLD

One of the major purposes of the amended Articles is to diminish the role of gold as a means of financial settlements between nations. The aim is to reduce the uses to which it is put in international monetary exchanges, and to eliminate it even as an international measure of value. Gold will no longer be used to express the value of a currency or of SDRs, the new reserve asset. There will no longer be an official price of gold; instead, it is allowed to find its own level in the world market. The requirement for member countries to contribute part of their payments to the IMF in gold is scrapped. Perhaps the most dramatic of IMF's steps to demonetize gold have been its actions to (i) return one-sixth of its holdings in gold to member countries, (ii) to auction off another sixth of its stock. The proceeds from these auctions (to continue over a four-year period) will benefit developing countries with particularly low *per capita* incomes.

SPECIAL DRAWING RIGHTS

Hand in hand with the de-emphasizing of gold goes effort to give greater status to the IMF's Special Drawing Rights, the new reserve asset which, it is hoped, will eventually become one of the principal instruments in the settlement of international payments deficits and in the accumulation of national reserves. A number of restrictions on the use of SDRs are being lifted. Governments will be able to use SDRs freely in dealings among each other, and no longer need to show the IMF that they have a special need to do so. The Fund itself will increase the uses to which it puts SDRs. Moreover, the number of entities entitled to hold SDRs will be increased. They will still, however, all be public.

MODERNIZATION OF THE OPERATIONS
OF THE FUND

A number of steps are being envisaged to improve the operations of the Fund and to make it more useful to members. Some of them stem directly from the sale of gold. Part of the gold proceeds will go into a Trust Fund to provide assistance to developing countries. But some of the new liquidity acquired may be invested in interest bearing obligations of member governments, thereby adding to the Fund's income. If the additions to its resources warrant it, the Fund may some day even be in a position to add to its members' quotas, not by asking for new subscriptions, but by drawing on its accumulated surplus. A new effort will be made to put to more effective use *all* the currencies deposited in the Fund, even those that are not widely accepted in international trade. (Central banks of the countries of such currencies will be encouraged to exchange them for so-called "freely usable currencies" when the occasion warrants.)

CONTROL OF THE FUND

Several of the proposed amendments recognize that the Fund like other international institutions is entering a period of intense negotiating activity in which issues, once considered to be mainly technical, will take on increasing political significance. To deal with these matters it is proposed to create a new institutional mechanism known as the Council of Governors.

The Council, in the words of Dr. Johannes H. Witteveen, Managing Director of the Fund, "will have the function to supervise the management and adaptation of the international monetary system, including the continuing operation of the adjustment process and developments in global liquidity and in this connexion to review developments in the transfer of real resources to developing countries and to consider proposals to amend the Articles of Agreement". The Council members would be Governors of the Fund, ministers of member governments, or persons of similar rank.

Political forces are also at work in a modification of the weighted voting procedure of the Fund. A country's voting rights are proportional to its quota, which in turn is related to its share in total international economic activity. Under this system developing countries until now commanded only 28 per cent of the total votes. Under a proposed rearrangement of quotas, some reductions will be made in the votes of certain developed countries, those of the non-oil exporting developing countries will remain unchanged, and the votes of the OPEC nations will double from 5 to 10 per cent of the total. With this rearrangement the total votes of the developing countries would rise to 33 per cent, enough to give them at least a theoretical veto power over most operational decisions which require a 70 per cent majority. Industrial countries, particularly the United States, enjoy a similar blocking power on politically-weighted decisions which require support by 85 per cent of the total voting power.

The process of reform of the international monetary system can by no means be considered complete. It is envisaged as an evolutionary and continuing process, calculated to keep in step with a changing world.

THE WORLD BANK

Beginning operations in June 1946 with a capital base of $10 billion, the World Bank has developed into the largest source of funds for countries on the lowest rungs of the economic ladder. Its present subscribed capital of about $31 billion provides some 80 developing countries with their major source of external capital. The Bank and its two associated organizations, the International Development Association (which provides easy terms for the worst off) and the International Finance Corporation (which lends exclusively to private organizations) are key elements in the international co-operative effort at economic and social development. Their operations are directly aimed at economic development, loans being made only for productive purposes.

Speaking before his Board of Governors in Manila in October 1976, Robert McNamara, President of the World Bank Group, took a hard look at the issues facing those responsible for dealing with the problem of world poverty. "The blunt truth," he said, "is that absolute poverty today is a function of neglect—and of our neglect as much as of anyone's. For we here in this hall represent the governments, and the financial resources, and the international institutions best suited to end the curse of absolute poverty in this century." The responsibility for such an effort, he said, lay first with the governments of the poorest countries themselves; and over the past decade they had shouldered most of it, financing 90 per cent of their investments out of their own meagre savings. But, Mr. McNamara added, "they must make an even greater effort in the future. They have, after all, invested less than $5 billion annually in agriculture (only 3 per cent of their GNP and only 18 per cent of their total investment programme), less than $100 million in population planning, and wholly inadequate amounts in essential public services. And much of what they spent has benefited only a privileged few".

"Yet whatever the degree of neglect the governments in the poorest countries may have been responsible for, it has been more than matched by the failure of the international community to assist them in the development task," Mr. McNamara went on. "The external assistance needed by the poorest nations over the past few years to achieve reasonable rates of economic growth, and to move towards meeting the basic human needs of their people, has been within the ability of the wealthy world to supply. And it would have been available had the developing nations met the target agreed on in the United Nations in 1970, of contributing 0.7 per cent of their GNP as official development assistance (ODA)— and had 0.2 per cent out of this been earmarked for programmes benefiting primarily the absolute poor." But the target had not been met, "nor is there any present indication that it ever will be met". If present trends continued, the level would be 0.33 per cent by 1980—lower even than the present 0.36 per cent.

In recent years the World Bank Group has increased its lending very substantially. From an average per year between 1964 and 1968 of $1.2 billion (current dollars), its commitments have grown to approximately $7 billion in 1976. Over the same period the number of IBRD and IDA projects has grown from an average of 56 per year to 214 in 1976. But this growth, accompanied by inflation, has brought the Bank to a rather perilous situation. Mr. McNamara pointed out in Manila that "if steps are not taken—and taken promptly—to relieve the resource constraints facing the Bank, this record of growing assistance to the developing nations will come to an abrupt halt and one of the world's principal sources of development finance could find its scale of operations being steadily eroded in real terms". By 1985, he said, present trends could reduce IBRD commitments to no more than $3.9 billion.

To prevent such a contingency and to allow what he considers essential growth in the Bank's operations, Mr. McNamara is pressing for an increase in resources. He recommends action on two fronts, one calculated to help in the long term, the other by 1977. In the face of double digit inflation if operations are to continue to grow beyond the seventies, Mr. McNamara urges that the existing statutory ceiling on loans be raised. The Articles of Agreement require this ceiling at the level of the Bank's subscribed capital and retained earnings—about $33 billion now. Raising the ceiling would mean increasing the Bank's capital and this in turn requires study and negotiation on several matters, not least the budgetary costs to member governments.

The other recommendation by Mr. McNamara—plea would be a better word—is that developed countries agree on higher contributions to the IDA when they are called upon to "replenish" it for the next three-year period beginning in June 1977. At the Governors meeting last year he had made a similar plea but the results so far have not been altogether encouraging. While several governments have openly supported the proposal that replenishment of IDA funds be targeted at $9 billion, others have balked. "Despite meetings of the Deputies of Finance Ministers in November 1975, and again in February and June of this year, there is as yet no final agreement on the amount of the fifth replenishment," Mr. McNamara told the Manila meeting. "Moreover, the burden sharing arrangements (i.e. who will pay how much) have not yet been negotiated." The implications of this, he pointed out, were not happy. "There is no practical action available to repair the reduction in IDA commitment authority this year. But we can and must act to prevent a complete hiatus in IDA operations beginning June 30, 1977." Such a hiatus would be difficult to avoid if there was no agreement on the level of contributions at least 90 days before the deadline, i.e., by the end of March 1977. Failure to do so, Mr. McNamara pointed out, would be a "tragic irony" in the midst of a general effort to strengthen international economic relations. "Failure to support IDA will be interpreted—and not unreasonably—as a clear indication that the international community's concern for the poor is little more than empty rhetoric."

CHAPTER XIII

THE LAW OF THE SEA

The great 17th century jurist Hugo Grotius, considered one of the fathers of international law, postulated in his treatise De Jure Praedae (on the Law of Prize and Booty) that the resources of the sea, being inexhaustible, were open for unrestricted use by all nations. But time and technology have changed that comfortable notion. It is apparent now that the appetites of modern man are so voracious, and his capacity for poisoning his environment so great that wise management is necessary if these vast resources are to last.

The United Nations recognized the need to recast the law of the sea at least as early as 1958, when it convened a conference in Geneva with the participation of 86 states. At that meeting four international conventions covering the territorial sea, the high seas, the continental shelf and fishing and conservation of living resources were adopted. A second Geneva conference in 1960 failed, however, to produce any substantive agreement on the limits of the territorial zone and fishing rights. And there matters rested for more than a decade, until developments in marine technology and growing economic conflicts over the uses of the sea led the United Nations General Assembly to convene a third conference on the law of the sea.

The preparatory work for the Third Conference on the Law of the Sea was done by the Committee on the Peaceful Uses of the Sea-Bed and Ocean Floor beyond the Limits of National Jurisdiction. This Committee, established by the General Assembly in 1968, produced after more than five years of work, a six-volume report containing draft articles which were the original basis for the work of the Conference.

The Conference held an organizational session in New York in 1973 and convened its first substantive session in Caracas in 1974. There and at the subsequent sessions in Geneva in 1975 and in New York in 1976, the laborious task continued of creating a whole new body of law for the seas. Procedures were established to ensure the widest possible agreement. It was decided that all possible attempts at consensus would be exhausted before taking any votes; and on matters of substance a two-thirds majority would be necessary. There was general agreement on such procedures because it was recognized that the issues of the sea would see the disruption of the usual voting patterns and alliances within the world community. A whole new range of interests were involved in discussions on the seas—the lines dividing advantaged and disadvantaged were changed, land-locked states and island countries found themselves in different categories, those with technology and those without were in different camps—traditional positions and relationships had to be re-examined.

The Conference met again in New York from 15 March to 7 May 1976, and succeeded in producing a "single informal negotiating text" to serve as the basis of discussion at a later session from 2 August to 17 September. Among the new concepts included in the text are a 200-mile economic zone for the coastal states, a maximum 12-mile territorial sea and a new regime, the International Sea-bed Authority, which would regulate the exploitation of resources in the sea and sea-bed beyond national jurisdiction for the common benefit of humanity, particularly the developing countries. Bernardo Zuleta, the Secretary-General's special representative to the Conference, says that the nations of the world were accepting concepts that only a short time earlier would have been dismissed as "wild products of the imagination".

The first part of the negotiating text would establish the Authority to administer an area larger than the land and sea territory of any single state. It would carry into practice the principle that the high seas are the common heritage of humanity, and cannot be claimed by sovereign states or used for anything but peaceful purposes.

As proposed, the Authority would comprise an Assembly of all members, an executive Council of 36 elected from among the Assembly with due regard to geographical representation and expertise, a Law of the Sea Tribunal whose 11 judges could rule on disputes related to the convention, an Enterprise to conduct undersea mining and other activities in the area and a Secretariat to administer the daily work of the Authority. The exact structure of the Sea-bed Authority as well as the system for the exploration and exploitation of the sea-bed is being considered by the First Committee of the Law of the Sea Conference.

Meanwhile, the Second Committee ponders general issues arising from the law of the sea. The informal negotiating text provides for "innocent passage" through a 12-mile territorial zone, and through straits. It would also permit navigation and overflight, or the laying of submarine cables and pipelines, in a 200-mile "exclusive economic zone", within which each coastal state would enjoy sovereign rights over natural resources, economic activity and scientific research. The Coastal States Group at the Conference said this zone should be *sui generis*, i.e., neither part of the high seas nor of the territorial zone. A definition of the continental shelf extending to its edge, if that were further than 200 miles, was also part of the package the group wanted. All nations would still have free access to and use of the high seas.

The negotiating text also contains provisions for the exercise of sovereignty by archipelagic states over the waters connecting their islands, and others stating that land-locked or geographically disadvantaged states have the right of access to the sea, (although terms for exercising this right must be negotiated with the neighbouring states involved).

The Third Committee of the Conference has focused on the obligation of states to preserve and protect the marine environment, as well as on the jurisdiction of states over pollution control. Proposals would have the coastal states bound to enforce environmental standards at least as stringent as those generally accepted internationally. This Committee has also discussed key issues such as the extent to which marine scientific research conducted in the exclusive economic zone should require the consent of the coastal state as well as means to promote transfer of marine technology among nations.

A fourth section of the negotiating text, to supplement the dispute settlement machinery of the proposed Law of the Sea Tribunal, was prepared by Hamilton Shirley Amerasinghe of Sri Lanka, President of the Conference. States parties to the convention could have the option of submitting disputes to the Tribunal, the International Court of Justice, or to special five-member conciliation commissions or arbitration tribunals. There are also special procedures for disputes involving pollution, fishing or scientific research.

When the fifth session of the Law of the Sea Conference opened in New York, its President called it "not merely a crucial session but a critical one". He warned that unless sufficient progress were made, either to sign a convention or to place it close enough to reality to require only one further session, "we would have lost one of the greatest opportunities ever placed before us".

The Conference, which has now been in session for over 33 weeks, has scheduled a sixth session in New York for seven or eight weeks beginning on 25 May 1977.

Whatever the accomplishments of the Law of the Sea Conference, it should not be viewed in isolation, but as part of a large effort by the United Nations to move the world beyond old antagonisms, towards solution of the great common problems confronting us all.

CHAPTER XIV

TO BE CONTINUED...

With every passing day the list of meetings and conferences grows longer, for the subjects under discussion are complex and difficult. Like the god Janus of ancient Rome who gave his name to the first month of the Western year, each conference is two-headed, one face looking back into the past, the other to the future. They signify a process, a continuum of change. But negotiated change is proving so painfully slow when measured against the magnitude of the world's miseries that observers grow weary and question not only their value but that of the United Nations itself. They do not take into account the harsh realities in the play of international power, the fact that the world body can be no more effective than its members want it to be. And in a time when peace is only a precarious stillness kept by the balance of armed threats, the mood is cautious and movement slow in shaping what must be truly epochal changes.

Under such conditions it is no mean feat that the United Nations has got a dialogue going and in the process softened the harsh edges of international suspicion. Across unfriendly borders now there is growing recognition of the need for co-operation. The developing countries have indeed committed themselves to co-operation among themselves on a scope not imagined a decade ago; and developed countries increasingly feel the pressure to consider international co-operation and assistance a moral and material obligation to their own well-being. Throughout its history the United Nations system has been involved in multilateral assistance and co-operation programmes, and this concluding chapter looks at the impact on them of the global dialogue on creating a new international economic order.

Courtesy Angelo Lodigiani

NEW DIMENSIONS FOR UNDP

The world's most broadly based development organization, with offices in 108 developing countries, is the United Nations Development Programme (UNDP). Meeting in Geneva in June 1975, the Programme's 48-nation Governing Council endorsed a series of "New Dimensions" in technical co-operation designed to redefine the future role of UNDP. "The basic purpose of technical co-operation," the Council's decision said, "should be the promotion of self-reliance in developing countries, by building up, *inter alia*, their productive capability and their indigenous resources—by increasing the availability of the managerial, technical, administrative and research capabilities required in the development process."

The Council's action aimed at increasing the range and flexibility of the Programme. In contrast to past emphasis on inputs, it said, technical co-operation should be seen in terms of output or the results to be achieved. To this end, UNDP was asked to provide equipment and material resources where necessary and to adopt a more liberal policy towards financing local costs and personnel. The organization was urged to support programmes of technical co-operation among developing countries and to diversify the sources of its supply, particularly those from developing countries.

These New Dimensions in UNDP technical co-operation are designed to liberate the Programme's joint planning with Governments from the traditional project "package" of foreign experts, fellowships, equipment and government personnel. They allow programming and project support to range wider and more boldly on the basis of needed results, allowing greater responsiveness to the needs of countries in different stages of development. They seek to move the Programme beyond its traditional means of providing assistance, stressing innovative methods of designing and delivering UNDP assistance. In most countries UNDP Resident Representatives have already begun discussions with governments on how, or how far, the recommendations can apply. Least developed countries particularly have welcomed the new approach because it helps to overcome constraints caused by lack of local financial resources.

Among more advanced developing countries, on the other hand, the emphasis in UNDP assistance is already sometimes on equipment. In India, UNDP has provided a sophisticated computer for the National Centre for Software Development and Computer Techniques. Cuba's project for the industrialization of bagasse (sugar cane fibre) has an equipment component accounting for 90 per cent of the UNDP-financed inputs. In the entire UNDP country programme for Cuba, equipment alone absorbs 62 per cent of the available resources. Not surprisingly, then, in this category of countries the new flexibility on equipment inputs is seen as particularly useful.

Developing countries as a whole continue to express serious interest in more reliance on national capacities for carrying out UNDP-assisted activities. Algeria, Cuba, India, Tunisia, Turkey and Yugoslavia, for example, have had national project directors or co-ordinators for some time. Other countries (such as Venezuela and Malaysia) have expressed interest. Local sub-contracting is already operating in Argentina, Colombia, Ivory Coast and Mozambique, and is being proposed for others. This includes sub-contracting to national institutions to carry out research or experiments in applying new technology.

In other substantive ways, UNDP has been furthering the recommendations of the United Nations General Assembly's sixth and seventh special sessions in its project work and in such areas as the promotion of technical cooperation among developing countries (TCDC). In this connexion, the Programme's special unit on TCDC is sponsoring four regional conferences in Asia, Latin America, Africa and West Asia in preparation for a world conference on the subject to be held in Argentina.

In their efforts to implement a new international economic order, developing countries are also attempting to fashion new technologies that are more suitable for their socio-economic conditions, their cultural values and the unique styles of their development. In Latin America for example, the newly created Latin America Economic System (SELA), will foster the establishment of multinational enterprises in that region which, among other things, will produce and market indigenous technology. UNDP funded a study by Latin American experts for the creation of the know-how to produce and/or commercialize technology locally. The study suggested the formation in the region of multinational schemes to produce technology more apt for development and at a financial and social cost acceptable to the countries concerned. After offering preliminary suggestions on the financing, organization and location of such enterprises, the main part of the study cited nine sectors where technological enterprises could be developed: electricity, nuclear energy, metropolitan railways, forestry, matrices, bread making, petroleum, plastics and steel.

Because industrialized countries remain the major producers of technology, however, developing countries continue to rely on transnational corporations for their advanced technological needs. Unfortunately, when many developing countries negotiate with transnational corporations, they lack the resources possessed by representatives of transnational corporations. Complementary to UNDP efforts to assist developing countries in creating appropriate technologies are the training courses sponsored by UNDP to prepare government officials for negotiations with transnational corporations. One such training course, organized and financed by UNDP with the collaboration of the Institute for Latin America Integration, took place in Buenos Aires, Argentina from 19 April to 8 May 1976. Previously, UNDP had funded training courses in Zambia, Romania and India.

UNDP is bolstering project work in the field of international trade, especially with respect to UNCTAD's integrated commodities programme. It has provided experts to help the secretariat of the Union of Banana Exporting Countries (UBEC) and is helping to set up Jute International, another producer's association. UNDP is also helping developing countries to participate in trade with socialist countries by holding training seminars for their trade officials to familiarize them with the possibilities.

These and other UNDP projects directly related to the goals of the new international economic order are few when compared to the over 8,000 UNDP-sponsored projects in the classical mode of development, but they are significant in the direction they point to for future development efforts.

INDUSTRIAL DEVELOPMENT

One of the primary means by which countries "develop" is industrialization. The growth of modern industry has a revolutionary impact on all aspects of society, multiplying many times over the volume of production and calling into sharp question a range of pre-industrial values and structures. At present all developing countries together produce only 7 per cent of the world's industrial output. Their societies are largely agrarian and at a low level of productivity. To change this, to meet the demands of growing population, they have all sought to encourage the growth of the industrial sector in their economies.

The United Nations Industrial Development Organization (UNIDO) held a General Conference of its membership in Lima in 1975. From it emerged the Lima Declaration and Plan of Action which has as its primary aim the restructuring and redistribution of the world's industry. It seeks to encourage the processing of raw materials in developing countries rather than shipping them elsewhere; it seeks to diversify the industrial capacities of these countries, for many now can produce only a narrow range of manufactures. It seeks as the end result of all this a share for the developing countries of 25 per cent of world industrial output by the year 2000. To help in the massive job of study, consultation and negotiation which this would require, the General Conference urged that UNIDO itself be strengthened within the United Nations system by making it a Specialized Agency and that a new Industrial Development Fund be created to finance its operations.

UNIDO is now in the process of modifying an internal structure that for nearly ten years has served the essential function of dispensing technical assistance services in the industrial field, financed largely by UNDP. It is creating an adequate basis to allow it to co-ordinate the activities of all organizations of the United Nations system relating to industrialization, and to serve as a forum for consultations not only between governments but between industries and between sectors of industries. In doing this UNIDO can count on its experience in planning regional industrial co-operation schemes, in studying the feasibility and location of industrial growth, and in helping to set up joint ventures. It also has considerable experience in aiding economic co-operation schemes, particularly in the field of development and transfer of technology. Consultations at the sectoral level have already begun or will begin in the near future in the iron and steel and fertilizer industries.

ENERGY

If the plans for accelerating the pace of industrialization succeed, one of the most predictable effects will be a bounding increase in the demand for energy. At present, the main energy source for world industry is petroleum, and there is general agreement that at some time in the future this source will be exhausted. But if there is agreement on this there is total confusion as to when exactly or approximately it will happen. Estimates of known resources vary widely and are marked by many different systems of classification. What is worse, most of these estimates do not account for substantial changes in prices and technology.

In the face of such uncertainty there is more than ever a need for international standards and systems of evaluation, and increasingly a need to act together to prevent harm to the global environment from the creation and use of alternative sources of energy. The United Nations system deals with the problems of energy at several levels—it is working towards standardization of statistics, it is trying to match evaluations, and it is actively involved in planning for the future. In the town of Laxenberg, near Vienna, a meeting was convened in July 1976 as a first step in this comprehensive approach. Meeting under the auspices of the United Nations Institute for Training and Research (UNITAR) and the International Institute for Applied Systems Analysis (IIASA), the meeting brought experts and officials together for a valuable exchange of views and information.

In 1977 a major United Nations conference will meet in Salzburg, Austria, to discuss the other major issue in the energy field: the use of atomic power. During the last two decades four United Nations conferences have reviewed the scientific and technical status of the peaceful uses of nuclear energy. Since the middle of the 1960s however, and especially since the 1973 rise in the price of oil, the commercial competitiveness of nuclear power has become more evident; simultaneously there has been greater awareness of the risks involved in such use. The 1977 conference is directed towards those responsible for the development and implementation of energy programmes, planners, decision-makers and managers. It will be held under the auspices of the International Atomic Energy Agency (IAEA), the specialized agency within the United Nations system that has been keeping a careful watch on the development of atomic power and of its use around the world. It is expected that the conference will result in a global and comprehensive overview of the status and potential of nuclear power, with particular emphasis on limitations and constraints on its present and future use.

HEALTH

The year 1976 might very well go down in history as the year smallpox was wiped out on earth; and major credit for this will go to the United Nations specialized agency, the World Health Organization. At a cost of some $85 million (less than the $88 million cost of a single strategic bomber), the WHO waged a long and relentless war against one of the oldest diseases known to man and by late 1976 it was fairly certain that the world was rid of the pox, except perhaps for a few villages in a remote part of Ethiopia.

The success of this effort has not, however, led the WHO to declare unilateral declarations of war against the many other diseases that ravage the poorer parts of the earth. Instead, carefully analyzing the problems of the developing countries, the Organization has come to the conclusion, in the words of its Director General Halfdan Mahler that "the danger of ignoring our failures and learning only from our successes is that we may thereby lose hard won knowledge and waste scarce re-

sources. In the Malaria and smallpox eradication programmes we can
see instances of broad campaigns where WHO has learned from its mis-
takes and is continuing to learn from them. The main lesson learned is
that, in the fight against disease, too much emphasis must not be placed

Courtesy E. Gurova

on health technologies alone. What we can achieve in this field depends
directly on the level of economic development of the countries concerned''. Specific actions are required of the health sector, as of other
developmental sectors, Mr. Mahler says, ''but only an integrated multi-

sectoral attack will be truly successful. An independent approach is unthinkable: the various agencies and institutions involved must work closely together to make the most efficient use of scarce resources''.

Expanding further on this theme, Mr. Mahler points out that health and economic and social development in rural areas are closely inter-linked. "While there is certainly an absolute minimum amount of pro-duction and consumption resources without which it is impossible for a person or a family to survive, there are many people with more than this minimum who lack the ingenuity, knowledge, or organization to be truly healthy. Similarly, it is almost impossible to visualize how a group that is malnourished, suffering from the distorted physical and social devel-opment associated with deprivation, and possibly diseases, can cope with the strains and innovations that accompany the economic development process. The emphasis must vary according to the nature of the situa-tion; for example, in the onchocerciasis areas of West Africa the health component should be the trigger mechanism for change, while in some of the areas suffering from drought and crop failure or clearly unjust land distribution policies, action in other sectors must take priority. There are also many examples where no special problem is obviously dominant.

"Whatever the requirements of a particular community," Mr. Mahler says, "it is unlikely that an approach confined to a single sector will be successful... WHO is now fully aware of the need to join forces with economists, agronomists, water engineers, and community and rural developers, or, in other words, to team up with the United Nations, our sister technical agencies, IBRD, the regional development banks, and the equivalent components of national governments for a combined ap-proach.

"I have no doubt that such integrated activities are essential to solve this problem and yet I am conscious of the lack of success of many of our previous efforts. Despite these past failures, WHO must voluntarily and forcefully move in this direction for health reasons, but with care and proper thought. We feel confident enough to do so and consider that the climate of world opinion is now ready for such a move."

IN THE HUMAN INTEREST

During the course of this book we have considered many different aspects of the international dialogue. Most of them have been abstruse topics—international trade, transfer of technology, industrialization, and other complex problems of economic and social development. But in the final analysis they all boil down to simple individual problems: hunger, sickness, poverty and death on one side, the "good life" on the other. They are in fact the problems of individuals multiplied many millions, and it is important to keep this in mind when speaking of international relations as a whole: we are talking in the end of you and me, of people down the road.

Two conferences in the last two years have particularly underlined this aspect of international relations: the World Population Conference in 1974 and the Conference of International Women's Year in 1975. The first said firmly in its final declaration that people are the most precious resource any country can have—in effect saying that human interests should be paramount in the shaping of economic and social policies. This might seem to be something that did not require affirmation, but it is often the case that in the pursuit of economic aims human values do suffer. And if evidence is necessary one has only to look to the global inequality of women, the result of age-old economic and social pressures.

The Women's Conference had three themes: Equality, Development, Peace. There was a natural linkage between the themes, for without the equality of the sexes there could be no true development and without development there could be no peace. The linkage worked also in the reverse direction, as a spokeswoman for Cyprus pointed out: "Without peace any attempt at development or equality is futile. Lack of peace has reduced Cypriote womanhood to a figure of tragedy, deprived of life, children, home, property and work". The conference ended with a call for the next ten years to be International Women's Decade, a period of intensive action to bring women all over the world out of their long night of oppression.

In closing this book it is appropriate that we look to the future and that in the most understandable human terms, in terms of the world's children.

And the picture here is mixed. "If we try to evaluate the situation of children in developing countries during the past year, we see two different, almost opposite trends," says a UNICEF report issued in March 1976. "On the one hand, field reports indicate that the situation of children in many parts of the developing world has deteriorated further in

1975. The number of children suffering from severe malnutrition and growing up without adequate educational preparation for a decent life is clearly on the increase. But there are also encouraging signs that the downward trend has slowed and might soon be reversed. And there are numerous reports of government initiatives aimed at helping to offset the worsening situation of their children through specific actions toward meeting their most pressing needs, particularly in the form of services at the village level. Thus, the picture we get is one which raises both anxiety and hope.''

APPENDIX I

DECLARATION ON THE ESTABLISHMENT OF A NEW INTERNATIONAL ECONOMIC ORDER

We, the Members of the United Nations,

Having convened a special session of the General Assembly to study for the first time the problems of raw materials and development, devoted to the consideration of the most important economic problems facing the world community,

Bearing in mind the spirit, purposes and principles of the Charter of the United Nations to promote the economic advancement and social progress of all peoples,

Solemnly proclaim our united determination to work urgently for THE ESTABLISHMENT OF A NEW INTERNATIONAL ECONOMIC ORDER based on equity, sovereign equality, interdependence, common interest and co-operation among all States, irrespective of their economic and social systems which shall correct inequalities and redress existing injustices, make it possible to eliminate the widening gap between the developed and the developing countries and ensure steadily accelerating economic and social development and peace and justice for present and future generations, and, to that end, declare:

1. The greatest and most significant achievement during the last decades has been the independence from colonial and alien domination of a large number of peoples and nations which has enabled them to become members of the community of free peoples. Technological progress has also been made in all spheres of economic activities in the last three decades, thus providing a solid potential for improving the well-being of all peoples. However, the remaining vestiges of alien and colonial domination, foreign occupation, racial discrimination, *apartheid* and

neo-colonialism in all its forms continue to be among the greatest obstacles to the full emancipation and progress of the developing countries and all the peoples involved. The benefits of technological progress are not shared equitably by all members of the international community. The developing countries, which constitute 70 per cent of the world's population, account for only 30 per cent of the world's income. It has proved impossible to achieve an even and balanced development of the international community under the existing international economic order. The gap between the developed and the developing countries continues to widen in a system which was established at a time when most of the developing countries did not even exist as independent States and which perpetuates inequality.

2. The present international economic order is in direct conflict with current developments in international political and economic relations. Since 1970, the world economy has experienced a series of grave crises which have had severe repercussions, especially on the developing countries because of their generally greater vulnerability to external economic impulses. The developing world has become a powerful factor that makes its influence felt in all fields of international activity. These irreversible changes in the relationship of forces in the world necessitate the active, full and equal participation of the developing countries in the formulation and application of all decisions that concern the international community.

3. All these changes have thrust into prominence the reality of interdependence of all the members of the world community. Current events have brought into sharp focus the realization that the interests of the developed countries and those of the developing countries can no longer be isolated from each other, that there is a close interrelationship between the prosperity of the developed countries and the growth and development of the developing countries, and that the prosperity of the international community as a whole depends upon the prosperity of its constituent parts. International co-operation for development is the shared goal and common duty of all countries. Thus the political, economic and social well-being of present and future generations depends more than ever on co-operation between all the members of the international community on the basis of sovereign equality and the removal of the dis-equilibrium that exists between them.

4. The new international economic order should be founded on full respect for the following principles:

(a) Sovereign equality of States, self-determination of all peoples, inadmissibility of the acquisition of territories by force, territorial integrity and non-interference in the internal affairs of other States;

(b) The broadest co-operation of all the States members of the international community, based on equity, whereby the prevailing disparities in the world may be banished and prosperity secured for all;

(c) Full and effective participation on the basis of equality of all countries in the solving of world economic problems in the common interest of all countries, bearing in mind the necessity to ensure the accelerated development of all the developing countries, while devoting particular attention to the adoption of special measures in favour of the least developed, land-locked and island developing countries as well as those developing countries most seriously affected by economic crises and natural calamities, without losing sight of the interests of other developing countries;

(d) The right of every country to adopt the economic and social system that it deems the most appropriate for its own development and not to be subjected to discrimination of any kind as a result;

(e) Full permanent sovereignty of every State over its natural resources and all economic activities. In order to safeguard these resources, each State is entitled to exercise effective control over them and their exploitation with means suitable to its own situation, including the right to nationalization or transfer of ownership to its nationals, this right being an expression of the full permanent sovereignty of the State. No State may be subjected to economic, political or any other type of coercion to prevent the free and full exercise of this inalienable right;

(f) The right of all States, territories and peoples under foreign occupation, alien and colonial domination or *apartheid* to restitution and full compensation for the exploitation and depletion of, and damages to, the natural resources and all other resources of those States, territories and peoples;

(g) Regulation and supervision of the activities of transnational corporations by taking measures in the interest of the national economies of the countries where such transnational corporations operate on the basis of the full sovereignty of those countries;

(h) The right of the developing countries and the peoples of territories under colonial and racial domination and foreign occupation to achieve their liberation and to regain effective control over their natural resources and economic activities;

(i) The extending of assistance to developing countries, peoples and territories which are under colonial and alien domination, foreign occupation, racial discrimination or *apartheid* or are subjected to economic, political or any other type of coercive measures to obtain from them the subordination of the exercise of their sovereign rights and to secure from them advantages of any kind, and to neo-colonialism in all its forms, and which have established or are endeavouring to establish effective control over their natural resources and economic activities that have been or are still under foreign control;

(j) Just and equitable relationship between the prices of raw materials, primary commodities, manufactured and semi-manufactured goods, exported by developing countries and the prices of raw materials, primary commodities, manufactures, capital goods and equipment imported by them with the aim of bringing about sustained improvement in their unsatisfactory terms of trade and the expansion of the world economy;

(k) Extension of active assistance to developing countries by the whole international community, free of any political or military conditions;

(l) Ensuring that one of the main aims of the reformed international monetary system shall be the promotion of the development of the developing countries and the adequate flow of real resources to them;

(m) Improving the competitiveness of natural materials facing competition from synthetic substitutes;

(n) Preferential and non-reciprocal treatment for developing countries, wherever feasible, in all fields of international economic co-operation whenever possible;

(o) Securing favourable conditions for the transfer of financial resources to developing countries;

(p) Giving to the developing countries access to the achievements of modern science and technology, and promoting the transfer of technology and the creation of indigenous technology for the benefit of the developing countries in forms and in accordance with procedures which are suited to their economies;

(q) The need for all States to put an end to the waste of natural resources, including food products;

(r) The need for developing countries to concentrate all their resources for the cause of development;

(s) The strengthening, through individual and collective actions, of mutual economic, trade, financial and technical co-operation among the developing countries, mainly on a preferential basis;

(t) Facilitating the role which producers' associations may play within the framework of international co-operation and, in pursuance of their aims, *inter alia* assisting in the promotion of sustained growth of the world economy and accelerating the development of developing countries.

5. The unanimous adoption of the International Development Strategy for the Second United Nations Development Decade[5] was an important step in the promotion of international economic co-operation on a just and equitable basis. The accelerated implementation of obligations and commitments assumed by the international community within the framework of the Strategy, particularly those concerning imperative development needs of developing countries, would contribute significantly to the fulfilment of the aims and objectives of the present Declaration.

6. The United Nations as a universal organization should be capable of dealing with problems of international economic co-operation in a comprehensive manner and ensuring equally the interests of all countries. It must have an even greater role in the establishment of a new international economic order. The Charter of Economic Rights and Duties of States, for the preparation of which the present Declaration will provide an additional source of inspiration, will constitute a significant contribution in this respect. All the States Members of the United Nations are therefore called upon to exert maximum efforts with a view to securing the implementation of the present Declaration, which is one of the principal guarantees for the creation of better conditions for all peoples to reach a life worthy of human dignity.

---

[5]Resolution 2626 (xxv).

7. The present Declaration on the Establishment of a New International Economic Order shall be one of the most important bases of economic relations between all peoples and all nations.

2229th plenary meeting
1 May 1974

CHARTER OF ECONOMIC RIGHTS AND DUTIES OF STATES

On 12 December 1974, the General Assembly adopted the Charter of Economic Rights and Duties of States, contained in resolution 3281 (XXIX). It was adopted by a roll-call vote of 120 in favour to 6 against, with 10 abstentions. In the preamble of the resolution, the Assembly stressed the fact that "the Charter shall constitute an effective instrument towards the establishment of a new system of international economic relations based on equity, sovereign equality, and interdependence of the interests of developed and developing countries".

PREAMBLE

THE GENERAL ASSEMBLY,

Reaffirming the fundamental purposes of the United Nations, in particular, the maintenance of international peace and security, the development of friendly relations among nations and the achievement of international co-operation in solving international problems in the economic and social fields,

Affirming the need for strengthening international co-operation in these fields,

Reaffirming further the need for strengthening international co-operation for development,

Declaring that it is a fundamental purpose of this Charter to promote the establishment of the new international economic order, based on equity, sovereign equality, interdependence, common interest and co-operation among all States, irrespective of their economic and social systems,

Desirous of contributing to the creation of conditions for:

(a) The attainment of wider prosperity among all countries and of higher standards of living for all peoples,

(b) The promotion by the entire international community of economic and social progress of all countries, especially developing countries,

(c) The encouragement of co-operation, on the basis of mutual advantage and equitable benefits for all peace-loving States which are willing to carry out the provisions of this Charter, in the economic, trade, scientific and technical fields, regardless of political, economic or social systems,

(d) The overcoming of main obstacles in the way of the economic development of the developing countries,

(e) The acceleration of the economic growth of developing countries with a view to bridging the economic gap between developing and developed countries,

(f) The protection, preservation and enhancement of the environment,

Mindful of the need to establish and maintain a just and equitable economic and social order through:

(a) The achievement of more rational and equitable international economic relations and the encouragement of structural changes in the world economy,

(b) The creation of conditions which permit the further expansion of trade and intensification of economic co-operation among all nations,

(c) The strengthening of the economic independence of developing countries,

(d) The establishment and promotion of international economic relations, taking into account the agreed differences in development of the developing countries and their specific needs,

Determined to promote collective economic security for development, in particular of the developing countries, with strict respect for the sovereign equality of each State and through the co-operation of the entire international community,

Considering that genuine co-operation among States, based on joint consideration of and concerted action regarding international economic problems, is essential for fulfilling the international community's common desire to achieve a just and rational development of all parts of the world,

Stressing the importance of ensuring appropriate conditions for the conduct of normal economic relations among all States, irrespective of differences in social and economic systems, and for the full respect for the rights of all peoples, as well as the strengthening of instruments of international economic co-operation as means for the consolidation of peace for the benefit of all,

Convinced of the need to develop a system of international economic relations on the basis of sovereign equality, mutual and equitable benefit and the close interrelationship of the interests of all States,

Reiterating that the responsibility for the development of every country rests primarily upon itself but that concomitant and effective international co-operation is an essential factor for the full achievement of its own development goals,

Firmly convinced of the urgent need to evolve a substantially improved system of international economic relations,

Solemnly adopts the present Charter of Economic Rights and Duties of States.

CHAPTER I
FUNDAMENTALS OF INTERNATIONAL ECONOMIC RELATIONS

Economic as well as political and other relations among States shall be governed, *inter alia*, by the following principles:

(a) Sovereignty, territorial integrity and political independence of States;

(b) Sovereign equality of all States;

(c) Non-aggression;

(d) Non-intervention;

(e) Mutual and equitable benefit;

(f) Peaceful coexistence;

(g) Equal rights and self-determination of peoples;

(h) Peaceful settlement of disputes;

(i) Remedying of injustices which have been brought about by force and which deprive a nation of the natural means necessary for its normal development;

(j) Fulfilment in good faith of international obligations;

(k) Respect for human rights and fundamental freedoms;

(l) No attempt to seek hegemony and spheres of influence;

(m) Promotion of international social justice;

(n) International co-operation for development;

(o) Free access to and from the sea by land-locked countries within the framework of the above principles.

CHAPTER II

ECONOMIC RIGHTS AND DUTIES OF STATES

Article 1

Every State has the sovereign and inalienable right to choose its economic system as well as its political, social and cultural systems in accordance with the will of its people, without outside interference, coercion or threat in any form whatsoever.

Article 2

1. Every State has and shall freely exercise full permanent sovereignty, including possession, use and disposal, over all its wealth, natural resources and economic activities.

2. Each State has the right:

(a) To regulate and exercise authority over foreign investment within its national jurisdiction in accordance with its laws and regulations and in conformity with its national objectives and priorities. No State shall be compelled to grant preferential treatment to foreign investment;

(b) To regulate and supervise the activities of transnational corporations within its national jurisdiction and take measures to ensure that such activities comply with its laws, rules and regulations and conform with its economic and social policies. Transnational corporations shall not intervene in the internal affairs of a host State. Every State should, with full regard for its sovereign rights, co-operate with other States in the exercise of the right set forth in this subparagraph;

(c) To nationalize, expropriate or transfer ownership of foreign property, in which case appropriate compensation should be paid by the State adopting such measures, taking into account its relevant laws and regulations and all circumstances that the State considers pertinent. In any case where the question of compensation gives rise to a controversy, it shall be settled under the domestic law of the nationalizing State and by its tribunals, unless it is freely and mutually agreed by all States concerned that other peaceful means be sought on the basis of the sovereign equality of States and in accordance with the principle of free choice of means.

Article 3

In the exploitation of natural resources shared by two or more countries, each State must co-operate on the basis of a system of information and prior consultations in order to achieve optimum use of such resources without causing damage to the legitimate interest of others.

Article 4

Every State has the right to engage in international trade and other forms of economic co-operation irrespective of any differences in political, economic and social systems. No State shall be subjected to discrimination of any kind based solely on such differences. In the pursuit of international trade and other forms of economic co-operation, every State is free to choose the forms of organization of its foreign economic relations and to enter into bilateral and multilateral arrangements consistent with its international obligations and with the needs of international economic co-operation.

Article 5

All States have the right to associate in organizations of primary commodity producers in order to develop their national economies to achieve stable financing for their development, and in pursuance of their aims, to assist in the promotion of sustained growth of the world economy, in particular accelerating the development of developing countries. Correspondingly all States have the duty to respect that right by refraining from applying economic and political measures that would limit it.

Article 6

It is the duty of States to contribute to the development of international trade of goods, particularly by means of arrangements and by the conclusion of long-term multilateral commodity agreements, where appropriate, and taking into account the interests of producers and consumers. All States share the responsibility to promote the regular flow and access of all commercial goods traded at stable, remunerative and equitable prices, thus contributing to the equitable development of the world economy, taking into account, in particular, the interests of developing countries.

Article 7

Every State has the primary responsibility to promote the economic, social and cultural development of its people. To this end, each State has the right and the responsibility to choose its means and goals of development, fully to mobilize and use its resources, to implement progressive economic and social reforms and to ensure the full participation of its people in the process and benefits of development. All States have the duty, individually and collectively, to co-operate in order to eliminate obstacles that hinder such mobilization and use.

Article 8

States should co-operate in facilitating more rational and equitable international economic relations and in encouraging structural changes in the context of a balanced world economy in harmony with the needs and interests of all countries, especially developing countries, and should take appropriate measures to this end.

Article 9

All States have the responsibility to co-operate in the economic, social, cultural, scientific and technological fields for the promotion of economic and social progress throughout the world, especially that of the developing countries.

Article 10

All States are juridically equal and, as equal members of the international community, have the right to participate fully and effectively in the international decision-making process in the solution of world economic, financial and monetary problems, *inter alia*, through the appropriate international organizations in accordance with their existing and evolving rules, and to share equitably in the benefits resulting therefrom.

Article 11

All States should co-operate to strengthen and continuously improve the efficiency of international organizations in implementing measures to stimulate the general economic progress of all countries, particularly of developing countries, and therefore should co-operate to adapt them, when appropriate, to the changing needs of international economic co-operation.

Article 12

1. States have the right, in agreement with the parties concerned, to participate in subregional, regional and interregional co-operation in the pursuit of their economic and social development. All States engaged in such co-operation have the duty to ensure that the policies of those groupings to which they belong correspond to the provisions of the Charter and are outward-looking, consistent with their international obligations and with the needs of international economic co-operation and have full regard for the legitimate interests of third countries, especially developing countries.

2. In the case of groupings to which the States concerned have transferred or may transfer certain competences as regards matters that come within the scope of the present Charter, its provisions shall also apply to those groupings, in regard to such matters, consistent with the responsibilities of such States as members of such groupings. Those States shall co-operate in the observance by the groupings of the provisions of this Charter.

Article 13

1. Every State has the right to benefit from the advances and developments in science and technology for the acceleration of its economic and social development.

2. All States should promote international scientific and technological co-operation and the transfer of technolgoy, with proper regard for all legitimate interests including, *inter alia*, the rights and duties of holders, suppliers and recipients of technology, In particular, all States should facilitate the access of developing countries to the achievements of modern science and technology, the transfer of technology and the

creation of indigenous technology for the benefit of the developing countries in forms and in accordance with procedures which are suited to their economies and their needs.

3. Accordingly, developed countries should co-operate with the developing countries in the establishment, strengthening and development of their scientific and technological infrastructures and their scientific research and technological activities so as to help to expand and transform the economies of developing countries.

4. All States should co-operate in exploring with a view to evolving further internationally accepted guidelines or regulations for the transfer of technology, taking fully into account the interests of developing countries.

Article 14

Every State has the duty to co-operate in promoting a steady and increasing expansion and liberalization of world trade and an improvement in the welfare and living standards of all peoples, in particular those of developing countries. Accordingly, all States should co-operate, *inter alia*, towards the progressive dismantling of obstacles to trade and the improvement of the international framework for the conduct of world trade and, to these ends, co-ordinated efforts shall be made to solve in an equitable way the trade problems of all countries, taking into account the specific trade problems of the developing countries. In this connexion, States shall take measures aimed at securing additional benefits for the international trade of developing countries so as to achieve a substantial increase in their foreign exchange earnings, the diversification of their exports, the acceleration of the rate of growth of their trade, taking into account their development needs, an improvement in the possibilities for these countries to participate in the expansion of world trade and a balance more favourable to developing countries in the sharing of the advantages resulting from this expansion, through, in the largest possible measure, a substantial improvement in the conditions of access for the products of interest to the developing countries and, wherever appropriate, measures designed to attain stable, equitable and remunerative prices for primary products.

Article 15

All States have the duty to promote the achievement of general and complete disarmament under effective international control and to utilize the resources freed by effective disarmament measures for the economic and social development of countries, allocating a substantial portion of such resources as additional means for the development needs of developing countries.

Article 16

1. It is the right and duty of all States, individually and collectively, to eliminate colonialism, *apartheid*, racial discrimination, neo-colonialism and all forms of foreign aggression, occupation and domination, and the economic and social consequences thereof, as a prerequisite for development. States which practise such coercive policies are economically responsible to the countries, territories and peoples affected for the restitution and full compensation for the exploitation and depletion of, and damages to, the natural and all other resources of those countries, territories and peoples. It is the duty of all States to extend assistance to them.

2. No State has the right to promote or encourage investments that may constitute an obstacle to the liberation of a territory occupied by force.

Article 17

International co-operation for development is the shared goal and common duty of all States. Every State should co-operate with the efforts of developing countries to accelerate their economic and social development by providing favourable external conditions and by extending active assistance to them, consistent with their development needs and objectives, with strict respect for the sovereign equality of States and free of any conditions derogating from their sovereignty.

Article 18

Developed countries should extend, improve and enlarge the system of generalized non-reciprocal and non-discriminatory tariff preferences to the developing countries consistent with the relevant agreed conclusions and relevant decisions as adopted on this subject, in the framework of the competent international organizations. Developed countries should also give serious consideration to the adoption of other differential measures, in areas where this is feasible and appropriate and in ways which will provide special and more favourable treatment, in order to meet the trade and development needs of the developing countries. In the conduct of international economic relations the developed countries should endeavour to avoid measures having a negative effect on the development of the national economies of the developing countries, as promoted by generalized tariff preferences and other generally agreed differential measures in their favour.

Article 19

With a view to accelerating the economic growth of developing countries and bridging the economic gap between developed and developing countries, developed countries should grant generalized preferential, non-reciprocal and non-discriminatory treatment to developing countries in those fields of international economic co-operation where it may be feasible.

Article 20

Developing countries should, in their efforts to increase their over-all trade, give due attention to the possibility of expanding their trade with socialist countries, by granting to these countries conditions for trade not inferior to those granted normally to the developed market economy countries.

Article 21

Developing countries should endeavour to promote the expansion of their mutual trade and to this end may, in accordance with the existing and evolving provisions and procedures of international agreements where applicable, grant trade preferences to other developing countries without being obliged to extend such preferences to developed countries, provided these arrangements do not constitute an impediment to general trade liberalization and expansion.

Article 22

1. All States should respond to the generally recognized or mutually agreed development needs and objectives of developing countries by promoting increased net flows of real resources to the developing countries from all sources, taking into account any obligations and commitments undertaken by the States concerned, in order to reinforce the efforts of developing countries to accelerate their economic and social development.

2. In this context, consistent with the aims and objectives mentioned above and taking into account any obligations and commitments undertaken in this regard, it should be their endeavour to increase the net amount of financial flows from official sources to developing countries and to improve the terms and conditions thereof.

3. The flow of development assistance resources should include economic and technical assistance.

Article 23

To enhance the effective mobilization of their own resources, the developing countries should strengthen their economic co-operation and expand their mutual trade so as to accelerate their economic and social development. All countries, especially developed countries, individually as well as through the competent international organizations of which they are members, should provide appropriate and effective support and co-operation.

Article 24

All States have the duty to conduct their mutual economic relations in a manner which takes into account the interests of other countries. In particular, all States should avoid prejudicing the interests of developing countries.

Article 25

In furtherance of world economic development, the international community, especially its developed members, shall pay special attention to the particular needs and problems of the least developed among the developing countries, of land-locked developing countries and also island developing countries, with a view to helping them to overcome their particular difficulties and thus contribute to their economic and social development.

Article 26

All States have the duty to coexist in tolerance and live together in peace, irrespective of differences in political, economic, social and cultural systems, and to facilitate trade between States having different economic and social systems. International trade should be conducted without prejudice to generalized non-discriminatory and non-reciprocal preferences in favour of developing countries, on the basis of mutual advantage, equitable benefits and the exchange of most-favoured-nation treatment.

Article 27

1. Every State has the right to enjoy fully the benefits of world invisible trade and to engage in the expansion of such trade.

2. World invisible trade, based on efficiency and mutual and equitable benefit, furthering the expansion of the world economy, is the common goal of all States. The role of developing countries in world invisible trade should be enhanced and strengthened consistent with the above objectives, particular attention being paid to the special needs of developing countries.

3. All States should co-operate with developing countries in their endeavours to increase their capacity to earn foreign exchange from invisible transactions, in accordance with the potential and needs of each developing country and consistent with the objectives mentioned above.

Article 28

All States have the duty to co-operate in achieving adjustments in the prices of exports of developing countries in relation to prices of their imports so as to promote just and equitable terms of trade for them, in a manner which is remunerative for producers and equitable for producers and consumers.

CHAPTER III

COMMON RESPONSIBILITIES TOWARDS THE INTERNATIONAL COMMUNITY

Article 29

The sea-bed and ocean floor and the subsoil thereof, beyond the limits of national jurisdiction, as well as the resources of the area, are the common heritage of mankind. On the basis of the principles adopted by the General Assembly in resolution 2749 (XXV) of 17 December 1970, all States shall ensure that the exploration of the area and exploitation of its resources are carried out exclusively for peaceful purposes and that the benefits derived therefrom are shared equitably by all States, taking into account the particular interests and needs of developing countries; an international régime applying to the area and its resources and including appropriate international machinery to give effect to its provisions shall be established by an international treaty of a universal character, generally agreed upon.

Article 30

The protection, preservation and the enhancement of the environment for the present and future generations is the responsibility of all States. All States shall endeavour to establish their own environmental and developmental policies in conformity with such responsibility. The environmental policies of all States should enhance and not adversely affect the present and future development potential of developing countries. All States have the responsibility to ensure that activities within their jurisdiction or control do not cause damage to the environment of other States or of areas beyond the limits of national jurisdiction. All States should co-operate in evolving international norms and regulations in the field of the environment.

CHAPTER IV

FINAL PROVISIONS

Article 31

All States have the duty to contribute to the balanced expansion of the world economy, taking duly into account the close interrelationship between the well-being of the developed countries and the growth and development of the developing countries, and the fact that the prosperity of the international community as a whole depends upon the prosperity of its constituent parts.

Article 32

No State may use or encourage the use of economic, political or any other type of measures to coerce another State in order to obtain from it the subordination of the exercise of its sovereign rights.

Article 33

1. Nothing in the present Charter shall be construed as impairing or derogating from the provisions of the Charter of the United Nations or actions taken in pursuance thereof.

2. In their interpretation and application, the provisions of the present Charter are interrelated and each provision should be construed in the context of the other provisions.

Article 34

An item on the Charter of Economic Rights and Duties of States shall be inscribed in the agenda of the General Assembly at its thirtieth session, and thereafter on the agenda of every fifth session. In this way a systematic and comprehensive consideration of the implementation of the Charter, covering both progress achieved and any improvements and additions which might become necessary, would be carried out and appropriate measures recommended. Such consideration should take into account the evolution of all the economic, social, legal and other factors related to the principles upon which the present Charter is based and on its purpose.

SCHEDULE OF UNCTAD MEETINGS
1976

	Date	Duration
First Preparatory Meeting for the Negotiation of a Common Fund	29 November- 3 December	1 week
Preparatory Meeting on Hard Fibres	6-10 December	1 week

1977

	Date	Duration
Preparatory Meeting on Rubber	17-21 January	1 week
Second Preparatory Meeting for the Negotiation of a Common Fund	24-28 January	1 week
Second Preparatory Meeting on Jute and Jute Products *a/*	31 January- 4 February	1 week
Intergovernmental Group of Experts on Copper, second session	7-18 February	2 weeks
Third Preparatory Meeting for the Negotiation of a Common Fund	21 February- 1 March	1 ½ weeks
Ad hoc Intergovernmental Committee for the Integrated Programme for Commodities, second session	2-4 March	3 days
Negotiating Conference on a Common Fund	7 March-1 April	4 weeks
Intergovernmental Group of Experts on Copper, third session	14-18 March	1 week
Third Preparatory Meeting on Jute and Jute Products *a/*	4-7 April	4 days
Second Preparatory Meeting on Copper	9-13 May	1 week
Fourth Preparatory Meeting on Jute and Jute Products	23-27 May	1 week

a/ At the level of governmental experts.

Preparatory Meeting on Tropical Timber	6-10 June	1 week
Preparatory Meeting on Manganese	13-17 June	1 week
Preparatory Meeting on Cotton	20-24 June	1 week
Preparatory Meeting on Vegetable Oils and Oilseeds	27-June-1 July	1 week
Ad hoc Intergovernmental Committee for the Integrated Programme for Commodities third session	11-15 July	1 week
Preparatory Meeting on Bananas	22-26 August or 31 October- 4 November	1 week
Preparatory Meeting on Tea	19-23 September	1 week
Preparatory Meeting on Bauxite	10-14 October	1 week
Preparatory Meeting on Iron Ore	24-28 October	1 week
Ad hoc Intergovernmental Committee for the Integrated Programme for Commodities, fourth session	28 November- 2 December	1 week 1 week
Preparatory Meeting on Phosphates	5-9 December	1 week
Preparatory Meeting on Meat	12-16 December	1 week
Other preparatory meetings and conferences	As required	up to 8 weeks

1978

Preparatory meetings and conferences	As required	up to 50 weeks

INDEX

110

OTHER TITLES OF INTEREST

The terms of our inspection copy service apply to all the above books. Full details of all books listed will gladly be sent upon request.